Fiscal Policy in Focus

The majority of economists today are opposed to allowing governments a significant role in economic affairs. In particular, demand management and redistributive policies are frowned upon, and supply-side policies (that concentrate on enhancing the profitability of business operations) are advocated as the only legitimate channels of government action. The possibility of 'government failure' in the economic sphere is endlessly emphasised.

The book argues that this view is only partially correct, at best. To make development inclusive and sustainable over the long run, the state must step in as an active enabler and regulator of private initiative. In a good society, the public–private relationship should be complementary, not adversarial. The enabler–regulator duty of the government cannot be effectively discharged with only supply-side and monetary instruments. Well-designed, effectively implemented fiscal action is indispensable for promoting social welfare with its twin aspects of efficiency and distributive justice.

Within a short compass, the strengths and limitations of tax expenditure policies in managing the economy are discussed in non-technical language, keeping the 'government failure vs market failure' debate as a focal point.

Soumyen Sikdar retired as Professor of Economics at the Indian Institute of Management Calcutta, India. He has also taught at Calcutta University, Burdwan University and Presidency University, India. As Faculty/Researcher, he has visited the Indira Gandhi Institute of Development Research (India), Osaka University (Japan) and Aarhus University (Denmark). His research interests include macroeconomics of open economies, India and globalisation and public policy.

Routledge Focus on Management and Society

***Series Editor: Anindya Sen**, Honorary Visiting Professor, Institute of Development Studies Kolkata (IDSK), India*

The aim of the Focus series is to present the reader with a number of short volumes which deal with important managerial issues in the Indian context. Volumes already published in the series cover topics which are of perennial interest to managers, like strategic change and transformation, and supply chain management, as well as emerging areas of research like neuro-marketing and digital culture. CEOs today also need to be familiar with critical developments in other fields, like auction theory and the contribution of sociology to management thinking. A forthcoming volume examines the law of one price in the context of dually listed shares, i.e., shares which are listed in both Indian stock markets and abroad. In other words, the Focus series is designed to introduce management theorists and researchers (as well as the general public) to a diverse set of topics relevant directly or peripherally to management in a short, readable format, without sacrificing basic rigour and set in the Indian context.

Indian Gold Jewellery Industry
Culture and Consumption
Sylvia Raha

Inequality, Economic Growth and Business Decision-Making
Asis Kumar Banerjee

Fiscal Policy in Focus
Responsibilities and Limitations of Governments
Soumyen Sikdar

For more information about this series, please visit: www.routledge.com/Routledge-Focus-on-Management-and-Society/book-series/RFMS

Fiscal Policy in Focus

Responsibilities and Limitations of Governments

Soumyen Sikdar

Routledge
Taylor & Francis Group
LONDON AND NEW YORK

First published 2025
by Routledge
4 Park Square, Milton Park, Abingdon, Oxon OX14 4RN

and by Routledge
605 Third Avenue, New York, NY 10158

Routledge is an imprint of the Taylor & Francis Group, an informa business

British Library Cataloguing-in-Publication Data
A catalogue record for this book is available from the British Library

ISBN: 9781032955421 (hbk)
ISBN: 9781032955445 (pbk)
ISBN: 9781003585404 (ebk)

DOI: 10.4324/9781003585404

Typeset in Times New Roman
by Newgen Publishing UK

In Memoriam

Birendranath and Kshetra Sikdar, my parents.

Contents

Acknowledgements

I have always been interested in the multifarious issues relating to the role of macroeconomic policies in the making of a good society. Aware of this, Anindya Sen invited me to write a short monograph on fiscal action in the Focus series he is editing. I am thankful to him for the offer. He also gave comments that improved the text, both exposition and content, in multiple places.

The ample resources of the library of the Indian Institute of Management, Calcutta, provided great help in the course of writing the book. The assistance of the library staff in locating the right material is gratefully acknowledged.

I record my appreciation of the effort put in by the Routledge team in giving the book its finished form.

Introduction

Visitors to Amsterdam sometimes wonder at the shape of the many tall and exceptionally thin buildings lining the famous canals. At the side of some of these buildings, hooks and hoist wheels are still visible, adding to the mystery. The cause can be traced to the Dutch tax on frontage or façade area. Owners wanted architects to do minimal frontage. Thin buildings could not have broad staircases, so an exterior hoist system had to be installed to bring furniture in and out of the higher floors. The majority of tourists, of course, are unaware of this.

In the celebrated Boston Tea Party of December 1773, more than three hundred chests of tea coming from England were dumped into the sea in Boston harbour. This action, which ignited the American Revolutionary War or American War of Independence, was a dramatic protest against enhanced tax on tea and other imports from England. (A popular cry of the revolutionary forces was 'no taxation without representation'. Representation meant membership in the British Parliament.)

The high cost of fighting the American War (1775–1783) forced King George III to impose a brick tax in 1784. Since each brick was taxed, producers switched to bigger bricks. The Crown responded by doubling the tax on bricks above a certain size. Some manufacturers went out of business, and there was a shift to timber and other materials.

In 1696, window tax (proxy for house size which, in turn, was proxy for the owner's wealth) of William III led to boarding up of windows in rooms deemed to be less important, thereby adding to the general gloom of British interiors. The tax was eventually repealed.

DOI: 10.4324/9781003585404-1

An earlier hearth tax (a proxy for family unit) had to be abolished, because attempts at evasion led to frequent fires.

Weight-based tax on glass in Europe in the early 18th century caused the introduction of smaller, delicate, hollow glassware known as 'excise glass'.

The famous Wat Tyler peasants' rebellion of 1381 in England was primarily a protest against a poll tax (fixed amount per head) on persons above the age of fifteen. Tax should be paid by rich landlords, not poor peasants, the rebels declared. The rebellion was suppressed, and Tyler was killed, but the tax was withdrawn. The necessity of the tax came from the long-drawn-out war with France.

The Jizya tax collected by Muslim rulers from non-Muslims for protection and permission to practise non-Muslim faith was also an annual poll tax. It proved to be an effective instrument for promoting conversion. Abolished by Akbar in India, its later reintroduction by his successors was the cause of several regional revolts.

Far down the timeline of history, in 2010 President Barack Obama of the USA stirred up a veritable storm by proposing to impose a tax penalty on those who refused to buy health insurance. It was finally accepted.

All these examples show the far-reaching effects of taxation imposed by rulers on their subjects through the ages. Consequences persist over centuries. The revenues collected were used to build roads, bridges, churches and palaces and provide other types of public services, but their most prominent use was the financing of wars, big and small, in which the kings and emperors of olden days were perpetually engaged. The great poet Kalidasa has some memorable words in this context: "As the sun receives moisture from the earth only to return it thousandfold, so did the king collect taxes to spend it for the benefit of his subjects". The poet here is praising the fiscal benevolence of his protagonist King Raghu, but in historical reality, in most kingdoms, most of the tax revenue has been spent on maintaining an army and conducting military campaigns for personal ambitions and aggrandisement of the rulers. Wars left their destructive legacy in history, while government-sponsored social projects like the construction of roads, railways and irrigation systems contributed to the welfare of current and future generations. We still marvel at Roman roads and aqueducts, the Chinese wall, the pyramids, the Taj Mahal and the temples, palaces and canals built by kings and emperors. Tax was ruthlessly extracted in the form of time and labour services and confiscated output of countless numbers of ordinary citizens.

The Netherlands in the 1500s provides a very interesting example of how taxation contributed to economic development in a big way. Much of the country lies at or below sea level. Early Dutch settlements acted in a communitarian spirit, with groups of residents supplying labour to the work of building and maintaining canals, dykes, dams and windmills to pump out water seeping into the lowlands. This kind of cooperative work to maintain and expand infrastructure came under strain during the planting and harvesting seasons. Instead of forcing citizens to contribute their time and labour, Dutch authorities authorised the drainage societies to tax residents and use the revenue to employ permanent staff to build and maintain infrastructure. Since payment in kind was not accepted, Dutch farmers were forced to sell their produce for money. The use of money in transactions spread quickly and played an important role in promoting trade and commerce. Thus, monetisation was promoted by taxation.

Plan of the book

Given the prominent role played by fiscal activities of the sovereign (kings in olden days, democratically elected governments of more recent years) and the importance of their consequences, there has been much discussion by thinkers on the multifarious issues surrounding such policy. Adam Smith enunciated canons of taxation and gifted the powerful metaphor of the invisible hand. Opinion on the proper role of the state in the economy and its size relative to private activities has undergone cycles, often influenced strongly by corresponding cycles in political philosophy or ideology. Evaluation of fiscal policy – the role of the state in general – has also displayed similar patterns. Buffeted by strong blasts from both the left and the right, non-specialist readers often lose sight of the central concerns. This short book is an attempt to help the reader – who may be a student of public policy, a doctor, a lawyer or a general manager of business or just an interested onlooker – to sort out the issues logically and form an informed opinion on them. Hopefully, this will make him or her a better citizen, with a greater capacity to participate in the democratic process.

The ideas to be taken up for discussion are laid out according to the following plan.

Chapter 1	Some important definitions and two divergent views
Chapter 2	Role of the state, notion of efficiency, types of economic policy
Chapter 3	How fiscal policy works
Chapter 4	Market failure and government failure
Chapter 5	Size of the public sector and costs of taxation
Chapter 6	Fiscal policy in global context
Chapter 7	Closer look at public debt
Chapter 8	Government actions for sustainable long-run growth
Chapter 9	Conclusion

1 Some important definitions and two divergent views

Fiscal policy (sometimes called discretionary fiscal policy) covers planned changes in the revenue and expenditure by the government. In modern times, these are normally set out in annual budgets, to which the media pay heavy attention and give extensive coverage. Many of the initial budgetary estimates are later revised.

- Budget deficit (BD) = government expenditure – government receipts
  (The opposite of budget deficit, the excess of receipts over expenditure, is budget surplus.)

Expenditures and receipts are broadly classified as two types – revenue and capital. *Revenue receipts* are of two types: tax revenue and non-tax revenue. The former can be broken up into revenue from direct taxes (personal income tax, wealth tax, corporate profit tax and so forth) and from indirect or commodity taxes (customs, sales and excise duties and so forth). *Subsidies* are negative indirect taxes. Under production subsidy, producers get more than the market price (market price plus the amount of subsidy) per unit of production or sale; under consumption subsidy, buyers pay less than the market price; the government makes up the difference to the sellers. Investment tax credit is provided to business to encourage capital formation in the economy.

Major items of non-tax revenue are earnings from public property – forests, mines, irrigation works, etc. – and earnings from public sector units (PSUs) and departmental undertakings such as railways, posts and telegraphs and interest on loans advanced. For almost all

DOI: 10.4324/9781003585404-2

countries of the world, including India, taxes contribute much more to total revenue than non-tax sources.

Capital receipts consist of borrowing from the public (domestic and foreign), small savings, provident funds, recovery of past loans and revenue from sale of equities (disinvestment) in PSUs. The interest paid on public borrowing goes into expenditure in the revenue account.

Borrowing adds to government's debt, better known as public debt. *Non-debt-creating capital receipts* consist of recovery of loans and PSU disinvestment.

The major items of *revenue expenditure* are civil administration including salaries and pensions, defence, grants to states and union territories and interest on public debt. *Capital expenditures* are spending on asset creation for the nation (e.g. construction of or addition to roads, airports, telecommunication networks, railways, sea ports and post offices).

Modern governments also make transfer payments, which are not payments for any productive action in the current period. Examples include unemployment benefits and pensions to retired employees and interest on existing public debt. These are included in revenue expenditure. Interest payments, pensions, wages and salaries and transfers are examples of 'committed expenditure' as opposed to 'discretionary expenditure'.

A direct tax like income tax is proportional if the fraction of income to be paid as tax remains the same (e.g. 7 per cent of income irrespective of its level); it is *progressive* when tax rate rises with the rise in income (e.g. 7 per cent for annual income up to Rs 10 lakhs and 12 per cent for higher levels). So, the tax burden per unit of income is lower for a poorer man. On the other hand, a rich man and a poor man pay the same sales tax when they purchase a commodity. These are *regressive*, as against progressive, because the burden is heavier for the poor man. A poll tax (fixed amount per head) is the most regressive. Wat Tyler and his men were fully justified in opposing it tooth and nail.

Some related concepts of budget deficit are as follows:

- Revenue deficit (RD) = revenue expenditure – revenue receipts
- Primary deficit (PD) = non-interest expenditure – receipts

Thus, interest payment on public debt is excluded in calculating PD.

Net public debt equals gross public debt minus holding of financial assets (cash, bank deposits, loans to the private sector, holdings in public and private companies and foreign exchange reserves).

Budgetary figures are available in India for the central and the state governments separately and also for the consolidated government sector. A useful and widely used source is the Economic Surveys, published annually by GoI.

Bond as a financial instrument

A bond is a financial asset that promises to pay the holder a fixed amount of money (the principal) plus interest on it over the period of maturity of the bond. A borrower who wants to take a loan to be repaid after, say, five years, issues a bond with a maturity period of five years. The interest promised, called the coupon rate, is printed on the bond itself along with the principal amount. The buyer of the bond is supplying the loan equal to the principal amount at the coupon rate. Bonds are tradable assets that are regularly bought and sold in financial markets. Whoever owns a bond at a particular moment in time is entitled to the stream of interest payments over her period of holding the bond. She will get the principal amount also, if she holds it to full maturity.

By selling bonds, governments can raise the money to finance their deficit. The main buyers are commercial banks and large investment managers like pension funds. Public debt or national debt consists of the outstanding bonds that a government issued in the past and that have not been redeemed.

Government bonds (also called government securities or G-Secs) are attractive to savers because of their low-risk characteristics. Unlike a firm, a state usually doesn't go bankrupt. Nations command an enormous amount of resources: physical capital stock, natural resources and the value of their production units. They also have the power to tax. All this gives confidence to the investors that governments won't default on their debt. But such *sovereign default*, though rare, is not unheard of. In 1917, the new Soviet government stopped payment on debt incurred during the czarist regime. In 1982, Mexico declared that it would be unable to service its debt (payment of interest and principal on maturity). The debt-to-GDP ratio had become unbearable. Similar declarations were made by Russia in 1998 and Argentina in 2002. Greece was on the verge of default during the Euro Crisis.

Chapter 7 treats public debt in detail.

Market structure

Perfect competition (or competitive market) is a situation where a large number of 'small' firms interact, and there are no barriers to entry or exit of firms. The operational meaning of 'small' is that the firm, being an insignificant part of the market, is unable to influence the prevailing price by altering its level of production (supply). It is a price taker. In perfectly competitive markets, firms will have to be as efficient as possible (buying inputs at the lowest possible cost and extracting the maximum technologically possible output from its inputs, so that there is no wastage). Since there are a large number of firms and entry is free, the equilibrium price (where demand equals supply) will be such that the firms can only make 'normal profits' that only just allow them to stay in business. Super-normal profits will be competed away. Moreover, since all consumers will determine their demand for commodities in accordance with their personal preferences and finances, the set of outputs will maximise social benefit in the sense that no rearrangement of production or consumption is possible that will raise the utility levels of consumers for given sets of personal preferences and production relations. The invisible hand of free market achieves what is best for the society.

It can be shown that the pursuit of maximum profit will induce each firm to settle its production (and sales) at the point P = MC, where P is the price of the product that the competitive firm sells and MC is marginal cost – the additional cost of an additional unit of production.

When the price-taking firm sells an additional unit of output, P does not change (because the extra sale is too insignificant relative to the market). Therefore, in this case, P is also marginal revenue (MR) – the additional revenue earned by selling an extra unit.

Profit maximisation requires production to be at a level where MR and MC are equal. The logic is not hard to follow. If at a certain level of production MR > MC, then profit (excess of revenue over cost) can be raised by producing and selling one more unit. Conversely, if MR < MC, profit can be raised by producing one unit less. The saving in cost will be more than the loss of revenue. So, at the most desirable level of output, MR = MC should hold. Now, for a competitive firm, P and MR are equal. So its output choice is where P = MC. This is a special case where P does not change with sales.

For big firms (monopolies and oligopolies, for example), MR < P, because additional sale will bring down the price. So at the output levels where their profit is maximum, MR = MC, but P > MC.

For the efficiency of competitive markets, the following are critical: small firm size, free entry and exit, full information, prices same for all agents, consumers being the best judge of their own welfare and no externalities (to be explained in Chapter 4).

Two divergent views

Through the ages, thinkers have failed to reach consensus on the ability of purely private incentive-driven economic systems to deliver social optimality. On the one hand is the group who have almost complete faith in the beneficial power of unrestricted market forces. We choose to call them *conservatives.* The other group, the *liberals*, do not share that faith. While admitting the power of market forces, they nevertheless believe that without proper regulation and intervention, the outcome may fall far short of the social ideal. It is not surprising that the two groups offer divergent guidelines with regard to the right size of the government and the permissible limits for its interventions in the economic sphere. This will be taken up in more detail in Chapter 5. The deep divergence of opinion between the two schools, conservatives and liberals, regarding the need for intervention in free market systems, can be captured through metaphors. For the conservatives, the economic system is like a rocking horse. It may be buffeted by external shocks, but eventually returns on its own to the original state of rest (equilibrium). It is inherently stable. No external assistance is needed to calm it down. For the liberals, the economy is like a ship on a choppy sea needing careful navigation to be kept afloat and on course. It may not return to its original position or course after storms, unpredictable shifts in currents and other shocks, but under the guidance of the captain, it will continue its journey towards its goal. The role of the captain and his crew is crucial for the good performance of the vessel and the welfare of the passengers.

2 Role of the state and types of policy

The Latin word 'fiscalis' means 'relating to the public purse'. 'Fiscal policy' is the name attached to the tax and expenditure operations of governments. The general term 'public sector' may be more appropriate than 'government', but for the convenience of exposition, we shall continue to use 'government' to mean the set of rules and economic institutions that stand outside the private sector or the market. The market system is the web of mechanisms where private agents – mainly consumers and producers – interact to determine the use of scarce resources (inputs or factors of production – labour, capital, land and natural resources). Both sets of agents are actuated by self-interest, with producers' self-interest being equated to the maximisation of profits. Prices of goods, services and resources play a critical role in the process. Monetary returns to resources used in production determine the distribution of income. These returns are determined by demand–supply interaction in the markets for their services. Demand for inputs coming from producers is deeply influenced by the demand for commodities and services they help to produce. Commodity and factor markets are thus fundamentally interlinked. Producers are sellers in the product market and buyers in that of inputs, whereas the status is reversed for households, who earn income by selling factor services and use that income to demand commodities for consumption.

A particular pattern of resource use is said to achieve *allocative efficiency* when, roughly, there is no feasible alternative pattern that can raise the society's economic well-being. This requires the greatest possible output from the finite amount of resources available to the economy. Mainstream economic theory shows that under

DOI: 10.4324/9781003585404-3

certain conditions, allocative efficiency can always be attained within the market system involving only private consumers and producers. Government intervention in the form of taxes and subsidies is justified only when those conditions fail to hold and private markets are unable to deliver efficiency. The distribution of income going with allocative efficiency need not be optimal or socially desirable, but the mainstream view is to place this 'equity issue' beyond the purview of 'positive' scientific economics.

Most conservative economists avoid equity issues and prefer to focus on efficiency alone. This will be taken up in Chapter 4.

Role of the state–public sector

The private sector of an economy is characterised by the pursuit of self-interest without any explicit caring for the social good. Buyers will choose to buy or reject a product only if it is beneficial for them to do so; producers will invest in a project only if it has the potential to add to their profits, irrespective of any other considerations. The public sector, headed by the government, is defined by contrast. It exists to act in the interest of the society at large, including future generations, looking beyond private gains or losses. This is a caricature, no doubt, but not a bad description of the key difference for our purpose. For the purpose of this book, government is equated with the public sector and the market economy with the private sector.

The five main roles of the government may be listed as follows:

1. Allocation: For various reasons, the market economy may fail to achieve efficient allocation of resources. This is known as *market failure*. The government has to take corrective action.
2. Distribution: Efficiency in allocation does not ensure that the distribution of income is just or equitable. In market transactions, the rich with greater spending power have more 'votes' than the poor. So, the product mix is likely to be biased in favour of the rich. The government's task is to correct the imbalance by using taxation, transfers and provision of public services at affordable rates. Private enterprise may not be interested to supply some services. The state must step in (Chapter 5).
3. Regulatory: The government frames and enforces laws of contract, property and consumer protection in order that the market economy may function.

4 Stabilisation: The market economy driven by the actions of private agents is subject to ups and downs, called *business cycles*. Unemployment rises during recessions (downswings) causing widespread suffering, and inflation often becomes a threat in booms (upswings). The government tries to use the macroeconomic tools of fiscal, monetary and other policies to moderate the cyclical swings in GDP and prevent the twin evils of joblessness and inflation from getting out of control.
5 Sustainable growth: Even in a well-managed economy (allocation efficient, distribution satisfactory), where GDP is growing (the twin evils of unemployment and inflation under control), growth may not be sustainable in the long run because of the destruction of natural capital in the process. Future generations will suffer catastrophic damage to their well-being (Chapter 8).

Types of government action

Government's economic action is broadly classified under three major heads: fiscal, monetary and supply-side policies. The last is also known as 'competition policy' or 'structural adjustment policies'.

Changes in taxation affect consumer and business spending by changing disposable income or tax-adjusted profits, while government spending, being a big source of demand for the output of the private sector, has a more direct impact. Conservatives emphasise the negative impact of taxation on the incentives to work and to invest.

Monetary policy works by changing the money supply (volume of liquidity in the financial system) and the structure of interest rates in the economy. At lower interest rates effected by the central bank (easy money policy), loans for purchasing consumer durables and for carrying out business investment projects become less expensive and private sector spending is stimulated. The opposite happens when interest rates are pushed up under a tight money policy.

For the most part, both fiscal and monetary actions try to influence the level of economic activity by influencing the volume of spending by consumers, investors and the government. Tax cuts stimulate consumption spending by raising disposable income, government purchases are an important source of demand for the output of the private sector, and interest rate changes affect spending by changing the cost of borrowing. In contrast, *supply-side policies* concentrate on boosting output and employment by promoting competition, improving efficiency (cost reduction) and giving workers more incentive to work. The main elements are as follows:

1 Lower taxation of companies and workers to stimulate investment and incentive to work. Since lower taxation will cause tax revenue to fall, government spending (including subsidies) should be contracted to maintain budgetary balance.
2 Deregulation of the private sector and privatisation. This covers making the labour market more 'flexible' by removing minimum wages, reducing unemployment benefits and generally lowering labour's bargaining power to protect labour standards. The main idea is that higher profitability is good for everybody.
3 Removing all restrictions on free movement of commodities across national boundaries (open current account) and of cross-border flow of financial funds (capital account openness).

The supply-side measures outlined above coupled with the requirement of fiscal discipline (very low volume of annual budget deficit relative to GDP and low value of public debt relative, once again, to GDP) constituted the pillars of the economic reforms programme advocated by the World Bank (WB) and the International Monetary Fund (IMF), gaining great momentum in the late 1980s following the collapse of the erstwhile USSR. This combined package came to be known as Structural Adjustment Programme (SAP) of the Washington Consensus, because these two international financial institutions are located in Washington, DC. Western countries could impose their will in the board because of the weighted voting system with weights being determined by financial contributions. (The essays in Serra and Stiglitz, 2003, give an excellent overview of the multiple facets of the consensus.)

Representatives of developing countries pointed out that poverty and inequality are likely to increase as a combined effect of reduced government spending, including transfers and subsidies, lower labour standards, deregulation and privatisation which inevitably leads to higher prices. But this went unheeded. SAP was made mandatory as part of the conditionalities of assistance provided by the IMF or WB. Its advocates insisted that the costs are worth paying for improving efficiency and competitiveness in the global market. Higher growth of GDP will cause poverty to decline in the long run. The rising tide of prosperity will lift boats of all sizes without any partiality.

Following the adoption of widespread reforms mostly in line with SAP, growth has indeed been stimulated and poverty has fallen in both China and India, the two countries with the highest incidence of poverty in the world. However, inequality, estimated by a number of alternative measures, has increased in both.

It is to be noted that there is no watertight separation between fiscal and monetary actions. Fiscal manoeuvres can have monetary implications, as is the case when part or whole of budget deficit is monetised.

Evolution of thought on the role of the state, and fiscal policy in India

Effective deployment of monetary instruments presupposes the existence of a well-developed financial system supervised by a central bank. It is a relatively recent addition to the set of tools for managing the economy. The first central bank of the world was set up in Sweden in 1668, the Bank of England dates back to 1694, and the Federal Reserve System (the Fed) of the USA originated in 1913. (The Bank of England was privately owned until 1946.) For the most part of recorded history, government economic action meant fiscal action. Uses and abuses of fiscal powers figure prominently in the age-old debate of the role of the state in economic management.

Adam Smith in his magnum opus, *An Inquiry Into The Nature and Causes of The Wealth of Nations* (1776) (better known by its short form, *The Wealth of Nations*), reacted strongly against overactive intrusive state, which, under the baneful influence of the prevailing doctrine of mercantilism, equated national prosperity with running high trade surplus and thereby adding to the nation's stock of bullion or precious metal. Smith maintained that this view is fallacious. A nation's wealth improves not by acquiring more gold, but by better utilisation of its productive potential and of the available labour force. In Great Britain of that time, the economic system was operating far below its productive frontier, shackled by wrong policies at the national and local levels.

Mercantilists also favoured the formation of state-sponsored monopolistic firms in both domestic commerce and international trade. The idea was that a part of the huge profits generated could be taken away to enrich governmental finances. Smith was strongly opposed to monopolistic market dominance and championed the virtues of competitive forces as instruments of growth and distributive fairness.

In the context of overintrusive states, Smith enunciated his celebrated principle of the invisible hand, which states that in the absence of ill-conceived state intervention, self-interest-driven demand and supply forces of the free market will bring about what is good for the society. Through markets, people do social good by doing personal good for themselves. But Smith's free market is not an unregulated market where big sellers can manipulate prices or quantities to change the outcome in their own favour. (Grampp, 2000, contains a good treatment of Smith's position on a variety of important issues.)

Departing from Smith's broad vision and choosing to forget his emphasis on the regulatory role of the state in ensuring competition, the conservatives came to equate the invisible hand with minimal government.

Marx and his socialist followers did not share this faith in the power of free markets to produce the best outcome for the society, neither did the liberals. According to the Marxists, capitalism will self-destruct through ever-growing accumulation accompanied by falling rate of profits and growing immiserisation of the masses. Capitalism is not a system that can sustain itself over time. We shall not follow the Marxist line of thought further in this book.

Faith in the supreme power of the invisible hand, as interpreted by the conservatives, was rudely shaken by the Great Depression that started with the stock market crash in the USA in 1929. The great work by John Maynard Keynes, *The General Theory of Employment Interest and Money*, appeared in 1936. It marked the birth of modern macroeconomics and in clear terms set out the justification for state intervention to fight recessions. In particular, it averred that in its rescue act the government should not hesitate to violate the principle of 'balanced budget'. On 31 December 1933, Keynes wrote an open letter in the *New York Times* requesting President Franklin D. Roosevelt (elected in March of that year) to raise spending immediately – 'build more railroads, really anything would do, bury money in old mines and sell digging rights'. Discretionary fiscal expansion was the order of the day. With the financial system in complete disarray in the wake of the stock market crash and innumerable bank failures, business and consumer confidence was at the lowest possible ebb. In this situation, monetary action will not be effective. But budget deficit should not be permanent; it is to be reversed when normalcy returns. Cyclical balance (deficit incurred in bad times offset by surplus earned in good times) should be the target.

This view became the orthodoxy in the post-war years. The idea of the welfare state, which plays an active role in promoting social welfare, was almost universally accepted. But then several factors, of which the sharp spike in inflation of the 1970s caused by unprecedented oil price hikes, and the mounting inefficiency of the public sector the world over were the most prominent ones, induced a shift of opinion away from the welfare state. An influential group of economists in the USA led by Milton Friedman revived the idea of self-correcting markets governed by their version of the invisible hand. The state came to be viewed as a heavy burden on the back of private enterprise, the only source of dynamism in the economy. Fiscal prudence became the new mantra.

This change of opinion coincided with the political swing to right-wing ideology in many countries, especially the UK and the USA. President Reagan of the latter put special emphasis on getting the role of the federal government scaled down to the appropriate size for a 'proper market-oriented economy'. (He is alleged to have said, "The nine most terrifying words in the English language are: I'm from the government and I'm here to help".) Prime Minister Margaret Thatcher in the UK resorted to similar rhetoric and policies on a wide front. This became the dominant view everywhere after the fall of the USSR in 1989. Under the new conservative ideology, demand-side policies (fiscal activism, in particular) are ruled out, protecting and enforcing property rights, removing all regulations of private business and implementing supply-side policies to improve efficiency remain as the only tasks left for the government. It is asserted that flexible labour markets will take care of the problem of joblessness. In the case of Europe, rigid labour standards and generous unemployment benefits (that reduced the incentive to work) are identified as the root cause of secularly high unemployment rates.

The quarter century 1945–1970 may be called the Age of Keynes when government intervention mostly in the form of tax expenditure policy was very common in developing and developed countries alike. But thereafter the conservatives championing the virtues of free enterprise capitalism became dominant.

So strong is the revulsion against government's activism under the new faith that fiscal policy is virtually abolished as a policy instrument.

Maintaining high and stable employment, which was among the top priorities for the welfare state, has dropped out of the agenda of economic management. Price stability is now the sole aim, and the task of inflation control is entirely entrusted to monetary action by the central bank.

Frequency of economic crises with long bouts of high unemployment increased noticeably under the new dispensation of deregulation and privatisation. One major crisis after another occurred through the 1980s, 1990s and early 2000s culminating in the devastating Global Financial Crisis (GFC) of 2007–2009, the worst crisis to hit the capitalist world order after the Great Depression. Then, in 2020 came the COVID-19 pandemic. Interestingly and ironically, in each crisis, the government had to step in as the ultimate rescuer and large-scale fiscal stimulus was the tool universally used to steer the system to recovery. In each episode, the champions of free market maintained silence on the inherent stability of unregulated capitalism. 'Unfettered capitalism' seems to be running on the nice principle 'privatize the gain, socialize the loss'.

In the theoretical 'benchmark' world of the conservative economists, labour and commodity markets clear instantly through flexible wages and prices and government's role is very limited. But the real economy is a long way off the idealised benchmark, where a multitude of frictions prevent quick movements in wages and prices, and commodity markets are monopolistic or oligopolistic in nature. New Keynesian economists belonging to the liberal camp have demonstrated that in the presence of such frictions and market imperfections, discretionary policy regains power to affect the levels of production and employment in the economy. (For an excellent critique of the optimality properties of the benchmark model of free competition, see the first chapter by Stiglitz in Serra and Stiglitz, 2003.)

In the conservative view, business cycles (ups and downs in overall economic activities) are situations where firms and workers are confused by price or monetary shocks (unforeseen events). The theoretical prediction is that cyclical unemployment is produced when workers quit to look for better jobs. Unemployment is voluntary, and the labour market continues to be in equilibrium. Apart from its evident absurdity, this is impossible to reconcile with the evidence that the quit rate actually goes down in recessions.

Fiscal action is back in the discussion of economic policy as a stabilisation tool, but not in the old unrestricted form. Awareness about its limitations has grown over the decades. It is increasingly recognised that it has an important role to play in improving distributive justice and the sustainability of growth. Chapter 8 has the discussion.

The evolution of fiscal policy in India since Independence

The years 1951–1990 may roughly be taken as the plan period in India. During these years, there was a radical transformation of the structure of the economy with agriculture's share in GDP declining from 57 per cent in 1950–1951 to 31 per cent and that of industries and services rising from 14 per cent and 30 per cent to 28 per cent and 41 per cent, respectively. Growth in per capita GDP rose from the stubborn Hindu rate of close to 1 per cent to 2.8 per cent. This is all the more remarkable against the universal growth slowdown in the wake of the great oil shocks of the 1970s and 1980s and despite the sharp rise in the share of petroleum in our import bill. The main driver was the substantial rise in saving and investment. Public investment played a big role in capital formation, adding substantially to the stock of social infrastructure in roads, railroads, ports and irrigation projects. Public sector enterprises played a key role in the production of critical inputs like electricity, steel, aluminium, chemicals and fertilisers. As a source of assured employment at decent remuneration, this sector enabled the creation of an urban middle class with substantial purchasing power. Since import penetration for most non-essential commodities was kept very low with the help of high trade barriers, the domestic private sector could flourish. A wide array of subsidies (negative indirect tax) on fertilisers and other inputs into food production was instituted along with generous minimum support price (MSP) for some major crops. A comprehensive public distribution system was also put in place. Interest rates were kept fixed at low levels to keep the cost of borrowing low for business. The apex monetary authority, the Reserve Bank of India (RBI), mainly played a secondary supporting role. This was unavoidable given the narrowness and lack of depth of financial markets.[1]

However, all of this underwent radical changes in the sweeping economic reforms of 1991. The background to this watershed event may be briefly outlined. Serious disturbing features on the fiscal front had begun to emerge during the 1980s, culminating in the crisis of 1990–1991. RD and public debt rose rapidly during this decade. Domestic saving ratio (saving as a percentage of GDP) flattened out chiefly due to very bad performance of PSUs in respect of saving (generation of surplus or profits). Given the paucity of domestic saving, even moderate increases in investment required higher imports, thereby widening the current account deficit. Foreign exchange reserves dwindled to a level precariously close to zero.

The Gulf War caused oil prices to shoot up with a simultaneous drying up of remittances. The collapse of the USSR led to a sharp decline in exports to the Soviet Bloc, and this contributed to the impending payments crisis. However, they were the proverbial last straw. Fiscal mismanagement was the root cause. Over 1980–1990, annual average fiscal deficit (FD) and net RBI credit to GoI (monetised deficit) as proportions of GDP were 8 per cent and 2.1 per cent, almost twice their values over the previous decade. Due to a sharp increase in the risk of sovereign default, the country's global credit rating fell steeply leading to a corresponding increase in the risk premium demanded by foreign creditors.

To avert imminent disaster, India had to approach the IMF for loan and that came with strict conditionalities. Drastic economic reforms touching every sector of the economy followed. Fiscal prudence was set at the top of the agenda along with downsizing the public sector. Many industries previously reserved for the public sector were opened up to private business. In the financial front, amongst a vast array of measures, caps were put on GoI's power to borrow from the RBI. In the area of stabilisation, the new regime puts heavy stress on the avoidance of persistent deficits and piling up of debt. This is supposed to create an environment conducive to private investment initiatives and long-term growth. Efficiency considerations are assigned supreme importance, and distributional concerns have been relegated to the background.

Price stability is considered to be more important than full employment. Monetary policy has taken over as the primary instrument for tackling short-run business cycles. The main reason is the ease and flexibility of monetary measures compared with the difficulty and the lags involved in changing fiscal parameters. But this alleged superiority is an oversimplification, once the major limitations of monetary action are recognised (Chapter 3).

At the behest of the IMF, the GoI was forced to impose strict discipline on its fiscal operations. This bitter medicine was necessary to cancel the negative impact of serious fiscal mismanagement of the 1980s. Budget deficit as a proportion of GDP, which was showing a steady upward trend, seems to stabilise in the post-reform years. Unbridled surge in the RD, which is excess expenditure for current unproductive activities, was largely brought under control. Improvement in fiscal health, captured mainly by the BD-to-GDP ratio, and opening up the economy to more competition, both internally through deregulation and externally through a sharp reduction in import barriers (mainly import duties and quotas), bore fruit in the northward movement in credit rating by global agencies (Box 2.1).

Box 2.1 FRBM Act

Legislative mandate for fiscal responsibility came in the form of the Fiscal Responsibility and Budgetary Management Act of 2003. Its major targets were as follows: complete elimination of RD by March 2009 and reduction of FD deficit to 3 per cent of GDP by March 2008. GoI was also mandated to take appropriate corrective action in the case of RD and FD exceeding 45 per cent of the budget estimates at the end of the first half of the financial year.

Despite widespread scepticism that this would just be another piece of legislation that exists only on paper, the Act has in fact succeeded in curbing fiscal indiscipline of GoI to a significant extent. It was temporarily suspended after the GFC of 2007 and the COVID-19 pandemic of 2020, which called for significant tax cuts and escalation in public spending to counter the forces of global recession.

The years 2003–2008 were the period of successful fiscal consolidation. Over 2004–2007, budget deficit as a proportion of GDP declined from 4.5 per cent to 2.7 per cent. RD, in particular, dropped from 3.6 per cent to 1.1 per cent. The reduction in deficit (both total and revenue) was achieved at the state level too. In the indirect tax front, value-added tax (VAT) was adopted by the centre and the states in 2004. At the same time, sweeping measures were taken to improve direct tax administrations and to widen the tax base. Subsidies were not abolished, but they were rationalised and scaled down considerably.

The tax-to-GDP ratio improved from 9.2 per cent in 2003–2004 to 12.5 per cent in 2007–2008.

The National Rural Employment Guarantee Act (NREGA), adopted in 2005, promised minimum wage employment of 100 days in every fiscal year to rural households with unemployed members. This is an important example of redistributive fiscal activism.

The fall of the Lehman Brothers in September 2008 triggered the GFC that plunged the world into a deep crisis second only to the Great Depression in the scale of asset destruction and human misery. As an emergency measure, the trend of fiscal consolidation was reversed the world over. India was no exception. Spending on infrastructure, irrigation and rural employment was stepped up, and the cap on market borrowing by the states to finance capital expenditure was raised. The Central VAT was cut by four percentage points (excluding petroleum products). Some import duties were temporarily reinstated to counter the huge revenue loss that resulted. The Fiscal Responsibility and Budgetary Management (FRBM) Act was temporarily suspended, and budget deficit, which was 2.7 per cent of GDP in 2007, jumped to 6.2 per cent in 2009.

Before the global catastrophe, two significant events had happened locally with serious implications for governmental finances. They were as follows: (a) debt relief for farmers was announced in the Union Budget of 2008 (2009 was the election year for the country); (b) the Sixth Pay Commission Report, submitted in March 2008, was accepted by the centre and a number of states. This constituted a significant jump in revenue expenditure in the form of higher wages and salaries.

The pandemic that started in 2020 and paralysed the world for two years also called for drastic fiscal expansion. Once again, spending was stepped up, taxes was reduced or temporarily suspended, and subsidies were raised.

(The chapter by Raychaudhuri in Bhattacharyya, Ghosh Dastidar and Sikdar, 2022, is a good summary of the macroeconomic impact of the pandemic on the Indian economy. Reddy, Ray, and Valluri, 2014, provide a good assessment of post-GFC monetary and fiscal actions in India.)

In the post-pandemic years, fiscal discipline has been restored to a large extent. Budget deficit as a percentage of GDP has come down almost to its pre-crisis level. Both the ratios, direct tax-to-GDP and indirect tax-to-GDP, have shown a mildly upward trend since 2000.

Total tax-to-GDP ratio stood at 11.8 per cent in 2021–2022. There is much room for improvement here.

As part of the Digital India mission, GoI has launched several initiatives for making the tax system more broad based, transparent and modern. They include the e-filing portal, the Annual Information Statement and the generation of e-bills under the Goods and Services Tax (GST) introduced in 2017. In *The Wealth of Nations*, Adam Smith promulgated four canons of taxation: fairness (in line with the ability to pay), certainty (transparency, infrequent change), convenience (simple to pay and collect) and efficiency (least distortion). India has moved closer to fulfilling these criteria of good taxation, though much remains to be done. In particular, for the sake of fairness, the importance of regressive indirect taxation must be brought down significantly.

Note

1 Source of the statistics relating to the Indian economy given in this section: GoI Economic Surveys, RBI reports, various issues.

3 How fiscal policy works

Total spending on the economy's current output during any period determines its GDP for that period. It can be decomposed into four elements: consumption spending by households, investment spending by business (firms), government spending and net exports (NX). The sum is called aggregate demand (AD). This is the main determinant of the level of GDP, at least in the short run when supply-side factors like capital accumulation, labour force growth and technological progress may be taken to be unchanging. These variables are denoted by C, I, G, and NX, respectively.

Consumption consists of current expenditure on durable goods such as cars, refrigerators, laptops and washing machines and non-durable goods such as food, clothing, cosmetics and services such as education, medical care, haircuts and tourism.

Investment (gross) is the amount currently spent on adding to the stock of physical capital. Output held in stock for future sale is counted as inventory investment. Suppose that a company decides to hold 1000 bicycles (produced in the current period) in its warehouse. The value of these products will be counted as inventory investment and included in current GDP, although they are not sold this year. Subtracting the value of depreciated capital, we get net investment.

Government expenditure is the sum spent by the central and state governments on purchasing currently produced goods and services.

Exports consist of the sale of domestically produced goods and services, and imports consist of the purchase by domestic citizens of goods and services produced by foreigners. Hence, in calculating domestic GDP, the value of exports is included and that of imports is

DOI: 10.4324/9781003585404-4

subtracted. In other words, only NX is included. If this is negative, the country is said to run a current account deficit.

The value of GDP equals the value of total expenditure on the nation's production from different sources. Denoting GDP by Y, this gives the basic macroeconomic relation:

$$Y = AD = C + I + G + NX \tag{3.1}$$

The advantage of this formulation is that changes in GDP (and hence aggregate employment) can be traced to changes in some component or components on the right-hand side. It also indicates how demand-side policies, fiscal and monetary, affect output and employment by changing AD.

Fiscal action affects each term of AD. If G is increased, the impact is direct. If personal taxes are cut, disposable income, that is, income net of taxes, increases and C will increase, because disposable income and consumption expenditure are positively related. Cut in business taxes or increase in investment tax credit (subsidy on business investment) will stimulate I; higher import duties or larger export subsidies raise NX by boosting exports (X) and lowering imports (M).

Private investment involves undertaking projects which needs to be started now, but will produce monetary returns over a certain number of years (the lifetime of the project) in the future. Most projects are financed by using bank loans (and partly retained profits). Higher interest rates charged by banks discourage I by raising the cost of borrowing. A fall in interest rates is expected to have the opposite effect. On the returns side matters are bit murky. Future returns spread over five, ten and fifteen years are uncertain and essentially unpredictable, because of the possibility of political and economic upheavals. Estimates also depend on the prevailing mood of potential investors and their psychological optimism or pessimism about the future of the economies, national and global. Unforeseen events, like the Ukraine war or the Gaza conflict, can seriously upset carefully laid-out business plans. A sudden drop in I (cancellation or deferment of investment projects) can cause GDP to contract by lowering AD. In every crisis starting from the Great Depression onwards, it is private investment spending that has shown the sharpest decline. Equation (3.1) says that by raising G appropriately, possibly combined with tax cuts to stimulate C, the negative impact of falling G on Y may be offset. This, in very simple terms, is fiscal action in its *stabilising role*.

Attempt to boost AD by means of planned increase in BD (via higher G and/or lower taxation) is known as expansionary fiscal action or *fiscal stimulus*. When BD is brought down (lower G and/or higher T), it is contractionary fiscal action or *fiscal contraction*.

The impact on Y of a change in any component of AD is actually more complex than the simple summation expression of Equation (3.1). There are direct and indirect effects to be taken into account. Let's take the case where the government decides to spend more (without raising taxes, so that budget deficit is higher). This has a direct equal impact on Y through AD, but the process does not stop here. The initial increase in production that occurs to meet the higher demand from the government generates extra income in some industries; workers and profit earners raise their consumption spending, which in turn stimulates production (and income generation) in some industries, leading to additional spending and income generation and so on. The ultimate impact on output and GDP (direct plus indirect) is greater than the initial increase in government spending. This is called the *multiplier effect*.

In addition to the government spending multiplier (through G), there is the investment multiplier (through I), which could be triggered by a decrease in the interest rate engineered by the central bank. By making borrowing cheaper, this boosts investment spending which boosts production (and hence income) over several rounds, similar to an increase in G. The remaining item of AD, NX, can also generate the multiplier along similar lines.

For the value of the multiplier, the critical parameter is the marginal propensity to consume (MPC), which is defined to be the fraction of additional income that is spent by households on buying goods. A numerical example will make its importance clear.

Consumption spending is primarily driven by disposable income. The relationship, however, is not one for one. When disposable income increases (say, by Rs 100), consumption spending increases, but by less than Rs 100, because a part of the extra income will be saved. Following the income increase of Rs 100, if spending rises by (say) Rs 75, MPC is 0.75. Saving rises by Rs 25, implying that marginal propensity to save (MPS) = 1 − 0.75 = 0.25.

Suppose the consumption relationship is represented by the linear form: C = A + b (DY), where A is a positive constant, b is a fraction, and DY is disposable income (income less taxes plus transfers from government). A part of consumption spending will be independent of current disposable income. The constant A captures this part. The MPC is the fraction b. For example, for C = 10 + 0.75 DY, MPC = 0.75.

There is a simple formula for the government and investment multipliers in an economy where foreign trade is not important or where the current account is always in balance, so that NX = 0.

Total change in income = (change in G or I)/1 − MPC
= (change in G or I)/MPS

The expression (1/1 − MPC) or 1/MPS is known as the multiplier. Since MPS is a positive fraction, the multiplier is greater than one in value. If MPC = 0.75 and the increase in G or I is 100, the total increase in output after the working out of the rounds of higher income, higher spending, higher income and so on will be equal to 100/(1/4) = 400. For MPC = 0.6, the multiplier is lower, equal to 250. This inverse relation between the propensity to spend and the size of the multiplier is logically clear. A larger MPC raises AD more in each round, leading to higher production and income in each round and hence a higher total impact. Savings, taxes and imports are the major leakages that reduce the magnitude of the multiplier.

There is also a tax multiplier. A tax reduction raises consumption spending by raising disposable income, and this starts the multiplier chain. The value of the multiplier, however, is lower in this case. The reason is not difficult to follow. Suppose that MPC = 0.75. A tax cut of Rs 100 will cause consumption spending to go up by (0.75)100, and saving will go up by (0.25)100. The saving part does not contribute to the rounds of income generation. An increase of Rs 100 in G or I, by contrast, raises income by the full amount of Rs 100 in the first round.

For an economy engaged in foreign trade, a part of the increase in income in each round will have two leakages, leakage into taxation and leakage into imports. The expression for the multiplier in this case is 1/(MPS + MPI), where MPI is the marginal propensity to import (the fraction of extra income that is spent on extra imports). For example, for MPS = 0.25 and MPI = 0.05, multiplier = 10/3. It is to be noted that the import leakage has brought down the value of the multiplier from 4 to 3.33.

For the conservatives, saving is not a leakage from the income stream. For them, S and I are always equal in the market for 'loanable funds', another instance of the invisible hand working. Their analysis is summarised below.

Investors need funds for implementing potentially profitable projects. So, planned investment creates demand for loanable funds. The supply of such funds comes mainly from the saving of households. Saving is the excess of disposable income over consumption. Interest rate represents the return on loans to savers and the cost of funds to borrowers (investors). Increase in interest rate encourages more saving (out of a given level of income) and discourages investors' demand for loans. This is why S is upward sloping and I is downward sloping in Figure 3.1.

If the interest rate is free to move freely, its value will settle at level r_1, where S and I are equal. For $r = r_2 > r_1$, supply of funds exceeds demand, and this will cause r to fall; the opposite happens at $r = r_3 < r_1$. (Both S and I are influenced also by the level of national income or GDP. Figure 3.1 is drawn assuming income is at its full employment level.)

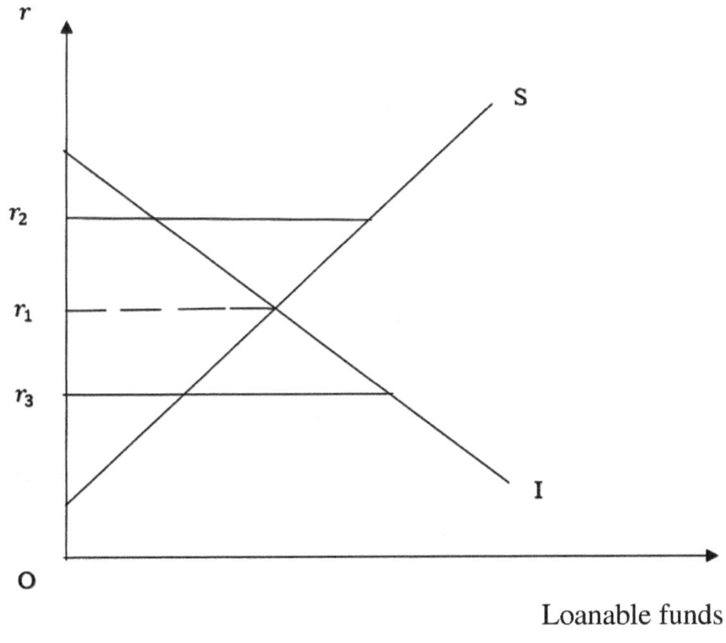

Figure 3.1 Loanable funds market.

Keynesians have objections to this reasoning. According to them, since saving depends on income as well as the rate of return, at the high full employment level of income, S is very likely to be higher than I and the gap may persist even at r = 0, the lowest possible value of the interest rate. In this case, the adjustment will be through a fall in the level of income itself, which will bring S down (leftward shift of the S curve). Demand–supply balance will be achieved at a positive interest rate, but the production level will be lower than the full employment level, and government action may be needed to push it up.

We have so far assumed a common MPC for all buyers, but in reality propensity to spend may differ across different classes of income earners. Poorer classes generally have a higher propensity to spend. This has implications for the impact of government action. A tax cut for the poorer households will stimulate consumption spending (and hence AD) more than a similar cut for the richer sections. Redistribution has an impact at the macroeconomic level. Suppose MPC of workers is 0.8, while that of profit earners is 0.6. If Rs 100 is taken away in tax from the latter, their C will fall by 60. If the collected amount of 100 is transferred to the former, their C will rise by 80. Net effect of this redistribution is to boost AD by 20.

Differing spending propensities also explain why rising inequality (with the income share of the rich rising at the expense of the poor) depresses the growth of consumption expenditure in the system.

Observations on the multiplier process

a As already noted, higher MPC raises the value of the multiplier. Saving is a leakage from demand, and therefore, a higher propensity to save depresses the process of income generation following any initial boost in AD. Consumption is a virtue when there is a lack of demand that is constraining output and employment.

b The multiplier cuts both ways. If instead of rising government spending or private I falls, income will fall to a multiplied extent. Contraction of demand will be passed on from one industry to another.

   Consumption is a relatively stable component of demand. Private investment, deeply influenced by expectations of business returns in the future, is much more unpredictable and volatile. The multiplier tells us that fluctuations in investor confidence have the potential to cause magnified fluctuations in today's output and employment.

c The operation of the multiplier is crucially dependent on the assumption that unutilised resources are available in abundance, so that production can smoothly increase in response to rise in demand without any upward push on the price level. The absence of supply bottlenecks is also important. If some crucial input, like petroleum or some metal or mineral, is in short supply, then the income generation process will grind to a halt as soon as that supply is exhausted. Further increases in demand will cause the prices of those limited inputs to rise with no change in quantity; this cost increase, in turn, will give a northward push to commodity prices. In other words, inflation will rear its head as a serious problem.

This will also be the outcome if in the initial situation the economy was at or close to the full employment output where all resources, including labour, are fully employed. Fiscal stimulus in this case will spend itself mostly in raising prices, with negligible impact on output and employment. New classical economists believe that because of perfect flexibility of wages and prices, full employment is a good description of capitalist economies. They, therefore, don't believe in the government's power to do anything positive by its demand management policies. Only supply-side interventions matter, in their view.

Tax multiplier may not operate if tax cuts are used by households to repay old debt. Current spending will remain unaffected in this case. A significant portion of the tax cuts in the USA after the GFC was utilised in this manner. Similarly, investment tax credit may be impotent to stimulate spending if pessimistic economic prospect, and not fund availability, is the major constraint on business investment.

In view of the preceding discussion, (1/MPS) is the maximum value for economies not engaging in external commerce, and (1/MPS + MPI) for economies open to trade. Actual values measured for the US and many European countries range between 1.2 and close to 2.

Observations on fiscal action in general

Although our extremely simplified analysis suggests that discretionary fiscal actions can be relied on to neutralise adverse changes in private spending, in practice no government is able to achieve perfect stabilisation due to the existence of various *lags and imperfection of information*. Even before taking remedial action, the policymakers first have to decide whether to respond at all.

Suppose that an economy that is reasonably close to full employment has been hit by an adverse demand disturbance or shock. The first problem is to distinguish whether the disturbance is permanent (expected to persist) or transitory. Suppose the shock is a one-period drop in consumer spending for some reason. It is transitory because consumption will revert to its original level after one period. In this situation, the best policy may be to do nothing and let the system recover on its own after the temporary setback. But compensatory action is required if the shock is expected to last for a significant period, in other words, if it is a permanent shock.

It is, however, not an easy matter to establish whether a shock is permanent or transitory. A major war, tsunami or earthquake unmistakably calls for immediate action. But in the case of the oil embargo imposed without warning by the OPEC in the early 1970s, it was by no means clear how long the embargo would last. Many experts at that time predicted that the newly formed oil cartel would collapse soon, and with the removal of the supply restrictions, the sharp spike in oil price will also be eliminated soon. In the event, 'soon' turned out to be more than a decade.

This problem facing the policymakers may be called the *recognition lag*. It is the period that elapses between the time a persistent shock occurs and the time the need for action is recognised. Two additional lags follow. *Inside lag* is the time delay between recognition of the need for intervention and the activation of the appropriate policies. *Outside lag* is the time lag between action and its impact on the economy.

Like the central banks of other countries, our RBI meets frequently to review the situation of the economy and decide on policy. Thus, once the need for action has been realised, the inside lag for monetary action is short. The outside lag is also short for such action. Evidence suggests that the inside lag in particular is longer for fiscal action because proposed changes in government spending and taxation require parliamentary approval. That is usually a lengthy process.

It should not be forgotten that monetary policy has timing problems too. Minutes of the Fed over 2006–2008 reveal that it took considerable time to recognise the seriousness of the downturn and to decide the magnitude of stimulus. There is also a significant lag between changes in policy interest rates and changes in private spending. In deep downturns, this transmission channel may not operate at all.

Returning to fiscal action, a long outside lag means that government intervention may end up actually destabilising the economy, because by the time the actions begin to be effective the economy may have moved out of the old phase into a new one because of changes in some internal or external factors.

To reduce the debilitating inside lag associated with fiscal action, automatic or built-in stabilisers have been devised. Such stabilisers do not require case-by-case deliberation or approval. Unemployment compensation is one important automatic stabiliser. In recessions, workers lose jobs and their consumption spending declines setting a negative multiplier into action. This can be offset to some extent if the worker receives unemployment compensation that will prevent disposable income from falling by the same amount as the loss in earnings.

Most developing countries do not have adequate unemployment compensation schemes in place. They have food aid or public works projects (National Rural Employment Guarantee Scheme in India, for example) instead. During economic downturns, these social safety nets go a long way to protect the standard of living of the vulnerable sections of the society.

Lack of information adds to the problem created by the presence of lags. Without a good estimate of the magnitude of the adverse (permanent) shock, the magnitude of corrective fiscal stimulus required is difficult to arrive at. Also, the values of crucial parameters like the MPC or MPI or the sensitivity of investment spending to changes in the costs of borrowing may not be precisely known. Hence, in the event of a change in I (actual or anticipated), it is far from easy to figure out the required compensating change in G and/or taxation.

As a result of all these factors, fiscal policy cannot be counted on to smooth out the fluctuations in GDP completely. It can, nonetheless, be a powerful tool for mitigating the severity of business cycles.

Expansionary fiscal action involves widening of the budget deficit in the first place. But the ultimate impact is lower because as income rises in each round of the multiplier process, tax collection (both from households and businesses) also increases. This is often lost sight of by people who are staunch and tireless opponents of fiscal activism because of its negative impact on deficit.

Debt monetisation and crowding out

An increase in G is called for to fight recessions. But how is this extra expenditure to be financed? Raising taxes is ruled out. In fact, taxes should preferably be cut to stimulate private demand. This leaves borrowing as the only means of finance.

The government may borrow from three sources: domestic citizens, foreign nationals and the domestic central bank. Of the three, the third source is special because it adds to the domestic supply of money. Unlike funds supplied by private lenders, the money that the central bank puts into the government's account as loan is new money. This is why the portion of government (public) debt financed by loans from the central bank is known as *monetised debt.*

Since debt monetisation has been widely practised in most developing countries, a few words on the special features of the device are needed.

First, consider the case when the government borrows from the public. Suppose Mr Desai lends Rs 1000 to GoI by buying a newly issued government bond of that face value and paying for it by drawing a check on his bank, Bank B. As Bank B's deposits fall by Rs 1000, its reserves at RBI are adjusted downwards by Rs 100, if the cash reserve ratio is 10 per cent. GoI spends Rs 1000 to buy goods from company X, which has an account at Bank C. As the money is deposited, Bank C's reserve at RBI must go up by Rs100. Total reserves (and deposits) of the banking system stay unchanged. There is no impact on money supply. However, when GoI borrows from RBI and spends Rs 1000 to buy from Company X and the money is deposited in Bank C, it is a net addition to the banks' deposits and reserves and money supply will go up through the standard credit expansion process. Government debt has been transformed into money. (The same logic applies if the central bank purchases other assets like gold or foreign exchange from the market.)

The resultant growth in money supply may cause inflationary pressures to emerge, if the economy is close to full capacity production or faces bottlenecks in the supply chain. Upward pressure on prices will, however, be absent in situations of deep recession.

During the plan period, GoI was forced to resort to large-scale debt monetisation as private saving was low and the market for government debt undeveloped. But this has been put under control since the reforms of 1991. The FRBM Act has played a big role in this.

Borrowing from abroad involves a drain on foreign exchange reserves because interest payment will have to be made in foreign currency. Depreciation of the home currency will multiply the cost of debt servicing. Chapter 7 has more on this. Even domestically held debt adds to the government's interest burden. In fact, interest on public debt is the largest component of current revenue expenditure of GoI, and it is growing. Debt servicing, however, may not be a serious problem because national governments have the power to tax, an instrument not available to private borrowers. The question of intergenerational fairness arises if future generations are taxed to service debt incurred in the current period.

Many economists contend that as the government steps up its borrowing in the domestic market to finance a fiscal stimulus, the interest rate goes up. In Figure 3.1, the demand for loanable funds shifts to the right, pulling up the market clearing rate from r to r. Private investment is discouraged as loans become costlier. Public spending *crowds out* private investment, which is bad for future generations as the capital stock they will inherit will be smaller.

New classical economists maintain crowding out as a strong argument against active fiscal intervention to fight recessions. But several comments are in order at this point.

First, it is wrong to suppose that saving or the stock of loanable funds will remain unchanged when G rises. As the multiplier process pulls income up, saving will also rise along with consumption spending by households. This will shift the S curve to the right in Figure 3.1, and interest rate need not rise or rise strongly.

Second, fiscal and monetary action may be used in combination. At the request of the government, the central bank may decide to raise money supply at the time of fiscal expansion. Essentially, this also boosts the supply of loanable funds in the system. This will prevent the interest rate from going up. Backed by this type of *accommodating monetary action* on the part of the central bank, higher government spending may not necessarily lead to crowding out.

Finally, the nature of public spending matters in an important way. If the higher G is for infrastructure investment in the form of building more and better roads, improving power generation and distribution capacity, irrigation projects and so on, the effect will actually be to encourage private investment. The relationship between public and private investment is often complementary, not competitive. There are numerous instances, in both India and other countries, which reveal that private investors show willingness to enter a particular area only after governments, local or central, have provided the necessary infrastructure like good roads, ports, uninterrupted power supply and telecommunication facilities. Just to give one example, in the USA, throughout the nineteenth century, investment in infrastructure like the Erie Canal and the railways was aggressively promoted by several levels of government.

If the higher public spending helps in creating socially useful capital, then actually crowding in, rather than crowding out, might occur. Private investment might increase despite a possible rise in the cost of borrowing. Crowding out is most plausible when the extra spending is pure consumption expenditure with no beneficial effect on social capital.

A famous instance where a major central bank refused to go for monetary accommodation is the action of the Bundesbank after the German unification of 1990. In an attempt to improve East German infrastructure up to West German standards, the West German government stepped up spending substantially within a very short period. This was accompanied by increased transfer payments to the citizens of former East Germany to raise their living standards. To avoid political unpopularity, taxes were not raised much, resulting in a sharp upward jump in budget deficit over 1991–1992. The Bundesbank, unwilling to give up its strong anti-inflation stance, refused to raise money supply to accommodate increased government spending. It kept money tight, and, as a result, interest rates in the country rose to levels not seen in decades.

Supply side and growth effects

In our analysis so far, fiscal policy affects production and employment by influencing AD. The supply side does not enter the picture because of the assumption of underutilised productive capacity and no supply bottlenecks. Demand is the sole determinant of output. An increase in demand will be met by an increase in production (through the multiplier process) without any noticeable increase in prices.

While this description might fit an economy in the grip of recession (low volume of production and employment), it has not escaped criticism in more general contexts. In particular, it has been asserted that taxation policy and practice may have important *incentive effects* on producers and workers. Higher taxation depresses production by discouraging people from earning activities. According to supply siders, tax cuts work as a stimulus not because consumption is boosted, but because people are induced to put in more effort and work more productively. More people may choose to join the labour force, thereby raising the Labour force participation rate (LFPR). But for these effects to be significant, the downward revision in tax rates must be substantial and believed to be permanent (non-transitory).

Effects of short-run fiscal action may have serious long-term consequences. Rising budget deficit implies rising cost of servicing a growing debt (repayment with interest). This may call for higher taxation of income and profits in the future. By reducing the expected levels of future profits, this may discourage current investment by business units. A lower BD, in contrast, may act as a signal of sound fiscal health, and this may have a favourable impact on growth by boosting the confidence of investors and consumers. High and persistent BD prompts a downgrade by global credit rating agencies, which will adversely affect the willingness of foreign investors to supply funds to the domestic economy.

All these implications, according to the new classical economists, should be kept firmly in mind while judging the efficacy of discretionary fiscal operations in the short run.

We return to the issue of BD and public debt in Chapter 7.

Fiscal activism and corruption

Historical experience shows that increases in government spending are often associated with the extension of political patronage and enhanced scope for corruption. Keynes broke with tradition that upheld the virtue of balanced budgets and boldly advocated budget deficit to pull the system out of the depths of recession. Unfortunately, politicians were not slow to exploit the legitimisation of budget deficits. Instances are legion in all countries, developed and not so developed, where lavish state-sponsored projects were launched regardless of their economic viability to improve the election (or re-election) prospects of influential politicians.

Market transactions, of course, are not dishonesty-proof, but the scope for malfeasance is greater in the public sphere because (a) officials and bureaucrats can in most cases escape punishment for harmful decisions, (b) accountability is low as cost of wrong decisions is usually distant and difficult to calculate at present and (c) losses caused by dishonesty or incompetence in PSUs can be passed off as the unavoidable cost of promoting the social good. Even honest officials may not scrutinise spending proposals carefully because they are dealing with other people's money.

Economists of the public choice school led by James Buchanan rue the fact that the balanced budget rule accepted in the American fiscal constitution has been destroyed by the acceptance of Keynes' fiscal activism. A fundamental asymmetry was blindly ignored in the naïve belief that politicians would create budget surplus in good times as willingly as deficit in bad times. The elementary rule is forgotten that politicians enjoy spending and do not like to tax.

Buchanan, Tullock and their followers have done a thorough analysis of what they call 'rent-seeking behaviour', where rent is any benefit obtained not productively but through influencing the decisions of policymakers. Larger and more powerful government bureaucracies, according to them, inevitably induce greater rent seeking which diverts scarce resources from productive use. (Buchanan, Tollison and Tullock, 1980, provide an excellent introduction to the literature.)

Fiscal consolidation may help in bringing down the level of corruption by blocking off some channels of socially unproductive public expenditure. After years of lax discipline, GoI now works under FRBM Act. This has yielded positive results, but there is much room for improvement yet.

Superiority of fiscal over monetary action

As an instrument for fighting downturns, fiscal policy enjoys a distinct advantage over monetary policy. Monetary easing – injection of more liquidity in the system – is supposed to stimulate spending (consumer spending on durables like cars and even houses and investment spending by business) by lowering the cost of borrowing. But when the economy is in recession, both consumer confidence and business confidence are at a low ebb and spending is unlikely to be stimulated even at a low cost of borrowing. Monetary action is thereby shorn of its wings. This has been borne out in every major downturns since the Great Depression (GD). During the GFC, interest rate was pushed down to a level very close to zero in the USA, Europe and Japan. But business was simply not interested to launch new projects. Households also decided to hoard the extra money made available by the central bank as an act of precaution against a potentially bleak and gloomy future.

Higher government spending, in contrast, has proved to be much more potent, being a direct addition to AD in the current period. This superiority, emphasised by Keynes back in the depression days of the 1930s, continues to be valid in the present scenario.

4 Market failure and government failure

Let us begin by stating the rationale for government intervention.

Intervention would improve allocative efficiency when the free market fails to attain that efficiency.

In the field of production, allocative efficiency requires that price (P) should equal marginal cost (MC), the extra cost of producing an additional unit of output. The logic is simple. Price is a measure of the consumer's willingness to pay for acquiring an additional unit of a commodity, whereas MC is the cost of producing that extra unit. If P is greater than MC at any level of output, society will benefit if consumers can have that unit, whereas in the opposite case of P being lower than MC, output should be reduced to raise social benefit. The optimal or efficient level of production is where P and MC are equal. P equals MC when the firm is maximising profit in perfect competition.

The situation where freely operating markets fail to deliver allocative efficiency is known as 'market failure'.

Four major sources of market failure are as follows:

A When big firms can affect the market price by their sales decisions. They are 'price makers' and not 'price takers'. The industry ceases to be competitive in this case. The bigness may be because technological economies of scale (where average cost (AC) falls as production expands) are so substantial relative to market size that a few big units can cover the whole market. Alternatively, the source may be restrictive trade practices collusively crafted by a few big producers. An industry dominated by a single seller is called a 'monopoly' and by a small number of large sellers, an 'oligopoly'.

DOI: 10.4324/9781003585404-5

It can be easily shown that under monopoly or oligopoly profit maximisation will cause production to be set at a point where P exceeds MC. Allocative efficiency is lost. Production is at a suboptimal level from the social point of view.

Corrective government action should be antitrust or price control (enforcing P = MC) if monopoly cannot be broken up. However, matters are not so simple. There are situations where the fixed cost of setting up business and starting production is huge, but the MC of producing additional units is small. In pharmaceuticals, the R&D cost of researching a new molecule is enormous, but the post-discovery production cost is relatively low. The situation is similar in the production of computer chips or new software and other items of knowledge production. The dominance of fixed cost will cause AC to decline with production, while low MC will keep it below AC. Enforcing P = MC mechanically in this situation will cause perpetual loss because price will fail to meet AC and strict regulation will kill the industry. To survive, the company must be allowed to charge price above its MC or receive subsidy from the state exchequer on a continuing basis. Figure 4.1 shows the per-unit subsidy needed if a declining cost activity is placed under price control. MC is taken to be constant for

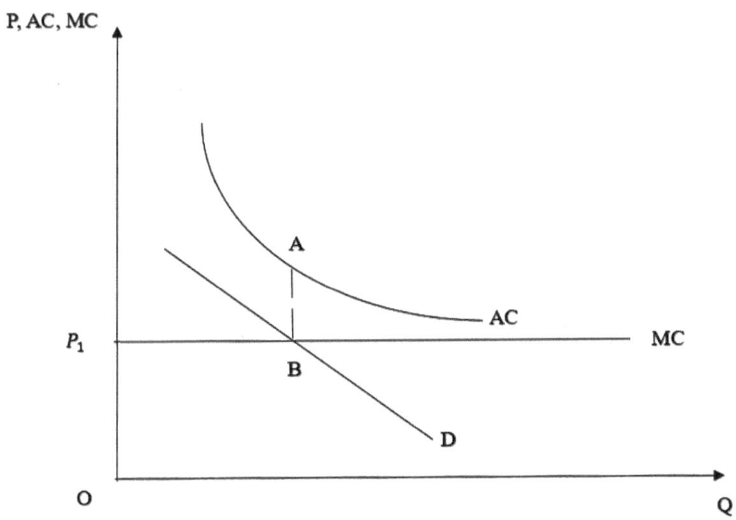

Figure 4.1 Subsidy in decreasing cost case.

convenience. Continuously declining AC (which stays above MC) is the crucial feature.

Socially optimal price P_1 (where the demand curve intersects the MC curve) is lower than AC at the corresponding level of output. It can be enforced only with a per-unit subsidy of AB.

To prevent the subsidy burden, monopoly or oligopoly (a small number of big firms) is often allowed to prevail in activities where AC decreases and MC is low. However, there should be regulatory oversight to protect the interest of consumers. This is why many pharma products are under price caps in several countries of the world including India.

B When social costs and benefits do not coincide with private costs and benefits. This is the case of externalities or external effects of consumption and/or production activities. These external effects lead to allocatively inefficient decisions even if perfect competition prevails in a market.

Harmful or negative externality

Driving a car may contribute to road congestion or road accidents or release pollutants into the atmosphere. This is a negative consumption externality that reduces the welfare of persons not directly associated with the buying and selling of that particular car. The factory that built that car also emitted pollutants in the process of production imposing disutility on the residents in the neighbourhood. This is a negative production externality. The MC of the car producer, his private MC (PMC), does not capture the social MC (SMC) that will put a value on the environmental damage inflicted by the car-producing unit. SMC > PMC here. Energy used by households, say, for heating, generates CO_2 which contributes to global warming which harms all living creatures of the planet. This is another instance of negative externality.

The socially efficient level of production should satisfy P = SMC, but left to their own devices competitive producers will continue to operate where P = PMC. Prices are therefore too low, and so production and consumption will be too high relative to the social optimum. Allocative inefficiency is the result. As a corrective action, government can do the following:

i Pass legislation to ban the activity causing negative externality. This draconian measure is inefficient because the socially optimal output level may be positive, not zero.
ii Regulate the activity by setting an upper limit to production at the socially optimum level.
iii Tax the negative externality, so that the producer's tax-inclusive PMC becomes higher and production is cut back. In honour of the British economist Arthur Pigou who was the first proponent of such taxes, these corrective measures are called Pigouvian taxes. While this is fine in principle, in practice calculating the appropriate amount of these taxes is far from easy. Required information on the damage inflicted on society and the culprit agent's private costs is generally not available to the regulatory authority. The practical difficulty of determining the right level of taxes was recognised by Pigou himself.

Government intervention has in principle the power to raise the welfare of the society. This is clear, but whether the government will have the incentive to carry out its task is another matter. If that incentive is absent, all the discussion of corrective action becomes of little value. This question is discussed below under 'government failure'.

Taxation and regulation are top-down solutions. The conservative economist Ronald Coase demonstrated that, under certain conditions, the problem created by externalities can be solved by private bargaining under appropriate assignment of property rights so that either (a) polluters will have to compensate those with a right to clean air or (b) those who want clean air will have to pay to prevent pollution. He showed that an optimal amount of pollution will result with either assignment of rights.

To understand the Coase argument, imagine the conflict between cattle rancher who doesn't maintain a proper fence between his land and that of a corn-growing neighbour. Cattle wander into the neighbour's land and damage the crop. Suppose that the value of the damage is Rs 100, while the cost of maintaining the fence is Rs 60. Fixing the fence would create the value of Rs 40 for the community. If the corn grower has legal right, the fence will be maintained by the rancher under threat of being sued and fined more than Rs 60. In the other case of the rancher having property rights, the corn grower would pay Rs 60 for the fence to be fixed. So, a purely bottom-up approach involving only the two concerned private parties seems to work.

But the conditions needed for this private arrangement solution are very restrictive. The 'transaction costs', the costs of finding the parties one has to bargain with and striking and enforcing the bargaining outcomes, are often prohibitive, especially if the number of persons involved is large. Proper valuation of damage may be problematic. Besides, clear assignment of property rights is often not possible for many types of environmental resources, such as clean air or sunlight. So, government intervention in the form of direct provision or restrictions (such as fishing or hunting limits) or imposition of taxes and subsidies is unavoidable.

Beneficial or positive externality

Market provision of a commodity will be too low when it has beneficial effects on third parties not directly involved in buying or selling. For example, my decision to get vaccinated at my own expense against a contagious disease benefits others because their risk of getting infected is reduced as well. Education helps the individual by enhancing her earning potential, but it has positive side effects for the society too. Educated mothers have fewer and healthier children. Higher education creates better citizens by improving their ability to think and act rationally. Because these positive social benefits do not figure in an individual's decision to invest in education based on private cost–benefit calculation, demand for education in a free market is likely to be too low relative to the social optimum. The government may justifiably use education subsidies to stimulate higher consumption. This is the reason why education, especially at the basic level, has been widely subsidised in so many societies.

Public goods

Public goods are characterised by two features:

(a) Non-excludable: It is not possible to prevent use by those who have not paid for the service provided. Examples are military defence, crime control and street lighting. Everyone benefits from street lights and safe neighbourhoods irrespective of whether they are local residents who have paid their taxes or visitors from other areas. The national defence case requires no explanation.

(b) Non-rival in consumption: One person's consumption of the commodity does not preclude anybody else's consumption.
The market demand curve for a private good can be obtained by summing the demands of the set of consumers, but such summation is meaningless for public goods as a given quantity can satisfy any number of consumers (up to a point at least, beyond which congestion may set in). So, the right approach seems to be to determine the quantity of the public good first and then charge each user her willingness to pay (a measure of the benefit she enjoys) for that quantity. However, once consumers realise that they cannot be excluded from the use of the public good, they will seriously understate their willingness to pay for it. They have incentive to take a 'free ride'. This will discourage potential private producers who will be unable to recover their costs. The market mechanism fails because of property (a). The government must step in as producer.

Many commodities have some of the features of public goods, but do not wholly satisfy (a) and (b). They are called impure public goods. For example, a public park may be non-excludable for all practical purposes, but too many users will spoil (b) by creating congestion. Hospital and education services are both excludable (to non-citizens, for example) and rival (there being a limited number of seats or beds, respectively). All this suggests that non-excludability and non-rivalness are not watertight categories. But the basic problem of cost recovery remains as a deterrent of market provision for services where elements (a) and (b) are strong.

Global public goods

Domestic public goods range from national defence, universal primary education to public health facilities, organic and inorganic waste collection and disposal to public swimming pools, parks and street lighting provided by local governments. But at the global level, there are public goods with cross-border character: their benefits accrue to countries and peoples, often across generations. Prominent examples include clean environment, lower global warming and a robust financial system. The major challenge of global public goods is that there is no world government to ensure their supply.

C Asymmetric information

Generally, sellers have better information about the product offered for sale than buyers. This may cause serious problems for the smooth functioning of markets. Think of used cars of two qualities – high and low. In a world where both parties have full information about the quality, some buyers will choose low-quality cars because they cost less, and others would prefer to buy high-quality cars at higher prices and all cars will be sold. The situation will change drastically if buyers are unsure about the quality. In this case, the maximum price the buyer is willing to pay, based on average expected quality, may fall short of the value that is acceptable to the owner of a high-quality car and some good-quality cars may remain unsold. All low-quality cars, however, may find buyers as for them the owner's acceptable value is lower.

A numerical example may be useful. Suppose that buyer's maximum offer prices are Rs 1000 for good quality and Rs 600 for bad quality; seller's minimum acceptable prices are Rs 900 and Rs 500, respectively. Under full information about quality, both types will be sold, as buyer's offers are acceptable to sellers. However, suppose that the buyer is unsure about the quality on offer and knows (or thinks) that only half the products are of good quality. Her offer price will fall to $\frac{1}{2}(1000 + 600) = 800$, at which price sellers of good quality will refuse to sell ($800 < 900$), but sellers of bad quality will still be willing ($800 > 500$). Market forces will fail to clear the market for good quality. Under Gresham's law, good coins are driven out of circulation by bad coins. A similar outcome prevails here due to the absence of full information.

The problem goes far beyond the case of used cars because the markets for insurance, financial credit and employment are all characterised by asymmetric information in different degrees.

To mitigate the problem, sellers often issue warranties. Government should maintain an effective legal system to ensure that those warranties are honoured.

D Coordination failure

The usefulness of driving on one side of the road is obvious to all. No conservative economist will object (and nobody has done so) if the government dictates which side it shall be. But a more interesting example may be given. Potential investors may be reluctant to set up a two-wheeler factory in a particular area if there is uncertainty about the supply of steel and tyres. At the same time, potential steel or tyre suppliers may be unsure about demand. The government may play a very useful role in bringing the two groups together for joint planning and may even provide some initial support with easy finance or assured purchase or other means. The Ministry of International Trade and Industry (MITI) set up by the Japanese government was responsible in a big way for coordinating the production and export plans of domestic makers of automobiles and electronic goods. MITI ensured that big Japanese corporations do not engage in wasteful competition among themselves in lucrative global markets. It is well documented that South Korea's spectacular post-1960 success owes a great deal to careful policy coordination involving the government on one hand and big business conglomerates (the chaebols) on the other.

Merit goods

Efficiency discussions assume that individuals are the best judges of their own welfare. But it is possible that they may undervalue the benefits derived from the consumption of a particular commodity or service. They are underestimating the merit of the good. For example, people often make insufficient provision for future contingencies involving ill health or injury. 'I should have saved more' is quite a common regret among retired persons. The returns from education are often underestimated, particularly by the poor and less educated groups. So, private demand for merit goods like health or accident insurance or education is likely to be biased downward from the social point of view. The government may (i) use compulsion (compulsory car or health insurance, for example), (ii) use improved information to help people make better judgements and (iii) encourage more consumption by providing subsidies to reduce the price paid by consumers (Box 4.1).

Both (ii) and (iii) have fiscal implications as they will involve higher expenditure on government account.

Box 4.1 Obamacare

To encourage the consumption of the merit good health insurance, President Barack Obama of the USA had the Patient Protection and Affordable Care Law passed in 2010. This is popularly known as Obamacare. The most controversial provision was that the absence of health insurance will invite a tax penalty. As many as twenty-six states challenged it as unconstitutional. The argument was that the government cannot force the purchase of insurance against will. The Supreme Court's verdict went in favour of the President. It declared that tax on remaining uninsured is within the power of the Congress. Without the mandate, the younger and healthier sections of the population would probably opt out, forcing the insurance companies to raise the premium and prevent universal coverage.

Government failure

Market failure arguments seem to demonstrate rather convincingly that government intervention in important areas is necessary to improve social welfare, but critics have questioned the ability of governments to do so. Two cases may be considered. First, the government understands what is to be done, but is not really interested to do so because of corruption in its ranks. A polluting industry may escape taxation or production regulation simply by paying suitable bribes. 'Government capture' or complicity between governments and big business is quite common in both developed and developing economies. Economists talk of markets all the time, but the very important and active market for political influence receives scant attention. Many companies regularly maintain armies of lobbyists to influence state policy. The public choice school highlights the phenomenon of government capture and is very sceptical of the government's ability to intervene fruitfully in a free market economy.

Second, even if the government is manned by sincere and honest persons, it may face formidable difficulty in carrying out its welfare-improving tasks because of the non-unavailability of relevant information. Finding the right amount of tax or subsidy to correct market failures caused by negative or positive externalities requires information about firms' cost structures, consumers' demand patterns and accurate values of social damage or benefit. This is a very tall order. Action on the basis of imprecise information may actually end up exacerbating the original problem. So, free market champions want a complete 'hands-off' policy on the part of the government. Both markets and governments may be imperfect institutions, but giving more power to the latter is, according to them, potentially more dangerous. The liberals hold the opposite view and maintain that the solution is to try to reduce the imperfection of the government. Because it has regulatory powers, a less imperfect government can do a lot to lower the imperfections of the private sector too. A government-bound hand and foot will not be neutral in its effect, and imperfections of the free market will increase by leaps and bounds. A most glaring example is the GFC that began with the collapse of Lehman Brothers in September 2008, second only to the GD in terms of destruction of assets and human suffering (Box 4.2).

Box 4.2 Global Financial Crisis

After the Great Depression, banks in the USA were put under strong regulation. Similar action was taken in Europe too. As a result, the frequency of banking crises went down remarkably. But under the widespread financial deregulation starting in the late 1980s, the regulatory framework was systematically dismantled, first in the USA and then in Europe. At the same time, securitisation led to the creation of ever more complex and non-transparent financial instruments which promised high returns. Banks and other financial institutions offered high-risk sub-prime products with ever-falling underwriting standards. Brokers were richly rewarded for duping borrowers mostly belonging to the poorer sections. Fund managers faced with complex, opaque instruments relied on credit raters (who suffered from conflicts of interest) or simply followed the herd.

Crisis followed when securities created out of mortgages on home loans (mortgage-backed securities) became worthless with the collapse of house prices (after a boom lasting six or seven years fuelled by very low interest rates) in the USA. The Lehman Brothers declared bankruptcy in September 2008. As the financial system was gripped by severe panic, interbank loans froze up, bringing the system into a free fall. The same story was repeated over much of Europe. Real GDP (and employment) underwent severe contraction in the majority of advanced countries. The following figures will give an idea about the magnitude of the damage.

In 2009, the percentage fall in real GDP was 3.5 for the USA, 5.1 for Germany, 4.9 for the UK, and 6.3 for Japan. For the first time since the end of the Second World War, global GDP actually shrank.

In every country, the government had to step in with massive fiscal stimulus measures. As conventional monetary policy was not working, unconventional measures like quantitative easing (QE) were undertaken by the Fed and other central banks to pump liquidity into the system and boost confidence.

There were clear warning signs of overvalued asset prices and highly questionable practices in the financial sector, but there was no regulatory authority to take preventive action. India escaped because, thanks to the vigilance of the RBI, banks did not have toxic assets in their portfolio.

While appreciating fully the weighty arguments of both sides of the market failure–government failure debate, we prefer to take a less partisan position. Lack of precise information and dishonesty of a section of the practitioners are besetting problems for many professions, including the medical and legal ones. But that should not lead us to conclude that society will be managed better if these professions are completely banned or severely restricted in their operations. That's a non-sequitur. The lesson is that governments should move with great care and caution in designing and implementing policies to correct market failure. In most cases, even partial correction may be better than no correction at all. Imperfect doctors, lawyers or teachers may still be better than no doctors, lawyers or teachers. Piecemeal adjustments on the basis of limited information have the potential to improve efficiency. Historically, subsidies for merit goods like universal education and taxes on harmful activities of various kinds have indeed succeeded in moving societies in the right direction. We agree with the words of the liberal economist Paul Samuelson, "The market system is the best system in the world. But without regulation it is a very bad system with tremendous built-in fragility". The devastating experience of the GFC is a testament to the truth of this in no uncertain terms.

Economists' notion of efficiency has no role for social or moral conceptions of *justice* or *fairness* of the outcomes of economic activities manifested in the distribution of income or wealth. Pro-market economists want to keep the subject 'scientific' and 'positive' by staying away from value-laden 'normative' issues of equity. This itself is a value-driven arbitrary imposition that can, and has been, seriously contested by liberal economists who maintain that efficiency should not be the sole criterion for judging the performance of an economic system. Fairness should be assigned due importance in assessing the overall welfare of citizens. Even if it does lead to some loss of efficiency, government intervention, according to this group of economists, is justified if it helps to bring about a more equal distribution of income, wealth and economic opportunities. Some broad measures of economic welfare revise GDP downwards whenever there is an increase in income inequality in a nation.

Just as the liberal school emphasises the role of distributive fairness in judging a society, the opposite camp is equally emphatic about the value of individual *freedom* in society. In the private sector, nearly all transactions are done on a quid-pro-quo basis, where costs and benefits are closely tied. This is not so in most transactions involving the government. Taxes are not collected from individuals on the basis of public benefits received, but on some other basis, usually the ability to pay as indicated by income or wealth. Whereas all private transactions are voluntary, most payments to governments are enforced by law. Coercion is needed because there is no direct link between benefits and payments. And coercion contradicts personal freedom.

This inevitable element of coercion is a major reason why the expansion of state activities is viewed as encroachment on private freedom and initiative by the conservative economists. History has shown that this coercion can fan out of the economic sphere to cover other aspects of the citizens' lives. The experience of post-Second World War Soviet-type socialism where individual freedom of action was mercilessly curtailed in the name of achieving 'collectively chosen goals' greatly enhanced this fear and mistrust of powerful governments. Governments inevitably tend to get bigger and bigger, and in the process, society is pushed closer and closer towards serfdom – this doctrine was set forth with great force by Friedrich Hayek in his influential book *The Road to Serfdom* (1944). Hayek quoted Leon Trotsky, the eminent communist leader, who had memorably stated, "Where the sole employer is the State, opposition means death by slow starvation. The old principle: he who does not work shall not eat, has been replaced by a new one: who does not obey does not eat".

What is our position here? We think that there is a need for a more nuanced and balanced approach. Just as we shouldn't over-emphasise the range of market failure, the putative conflict between public and private actions in the realm of freedom should also be viewed in a proper perspective. Suitable government actions that promote the access of citizens to health or education services or credit facilities, for example, may actually promote societal freedom by expanding the capability of the less privileged sections of the population to participate more effectively in the economic process. It is not hard to see, unless one is blinkered by ideology, that in highly unequal societies the rich have too much freedom and the poor too little in all spheres of decision-making. To quote the philosopher Isaiah Berlin, "Freedom for the foxes has often meant death to the sheep".

A prosperous society where the fruits of growth are equitably enjoyed by all sections may justifiably be said to be enjoying more freedom (to realise full human potentialities) than another one where income and wealth are mostly concentrated in the hands of a small elite. Freedom and exclusion (social, political and economic) are fundamentally contradictory.

This is squarely in line with Amartya Sen's idea of freedom presented in the book *Development as Freedom* (1999) and other works. He has enunciated an approach where well-being is captured by things people can do (their set of capabilities), rather than things people have. If the capability set expands, people can do more of the things they would like to do and their freedom will expand. Clearly, appropriately designed and implemented actions by democratic governments can go a long way in improving the freedom of the less privileged sections of the society.

There is another more mundane dimension to the issue. Even in advanced capitalist societies, government's cumulative investment over decades or even centuries in infrastructure building (not only the hard infrastructure of physical capital but also the soft ones like a safe business environment, security of private property and consumer confidence) is strongly complementary and not competitive with the interests of private business, which needs that infrastructure to operate on. Such complementarity is a great counterweight to the alleged curtailment of private freedom associated with government action. The public–private relationship is by no means always adversarial.

In the matter of promoting fairness, taxing the rich and subsidising the consumption of the poorer and less privileged sections of the population with the tax proceeds are easier said than done. The political clout of the wealthier sections often blocks these efforts successfully. Even in the absence of political manipulation, plain corruption also often results in the provision of public services of poor quality to the 'submerged part' of the society.

In Nigeria's capital city Lagos, access to piped water is confined to the middle-income and affluent households. The poor have to buy water from private vendors at high prices. Naturally, they often use illegal taps on makeshift pipes connected to water sources that are often contaminated. Local government agencies do not show any interest in addressing this basic problem. Lagos is by no means unique in this failure of public provision of an essential service. The story can be repeated for hundreds of large cities, small towns and villages in Asia, Africa and Latin America. But once again, this should be a spur for reducing corruption and improving the quality of governance in general, rather than an argument for a blanket ban on redistributive efforts of national and local governments. The baby must not be thrown away with the bathwater.

Box 4.3 The radical proposals of Thomas Paine

Thomas Paine (1737–1809), the influential revolutionary and political philosopher, was seriously concerned about the ill effects of distributional unfairness and advocated several radical plans for containing the trend of rising inequality of his times. These include the creation of a national fund to pay every young man and woman at age 21 a sum of fifteen pounds (not an insignificant amount at that time) to make a start in the world. On reaching age 50, persons will be entitled to an annual pension of ten pounds. An inheritance tax of 10 per cent of value of landed property on the death of the owner should be sufficient to fund the programme.

Paine was tireless in stressing the unjustified origins of landed property, but did recognise the contribution of landlords in raising the productivity of agricultural operations.

The Washington Consensus prescribed rolling back the frontiers of state action in every field. There has been a shift in policy from managing the economy to managing only the budget. The result, not unexpectedly, is an alarming rise in poverty and inequality. This, in turn, has resulted in a strong backlash against liberalisation and privatisation. It was promised that the rising tide of prosperity will lift all boats, big or small. That has simply not happened.

We shall end with a few words on the emerging branch of behavioural welfare economics. The theory of rational choice, which is the central pillar of mainstream economic theory, is built on certain 'rationality postulates' on individual's preferences. Rationality includes the power to figure out correctly the costs and benefits of alternative feasible actions. On the basis of accumulated evidence (generated both within and outside laboratories), psychologists and behavioural economists have questioned the validity of these postulates. They have demonstrated convincingly that individuals display systematic biases in their judgement and often make pretty bad decisions – decisions that they wouldn't make if they had possessed complete information, perfect cognitive abilities and perfect self-control. At best, in their terminology, human beings are *boundedly rational.*

According to behavioural welfare economics, in a society of imperfectly rational individuals carefully designed public intervention can improve welfare. The decision-makers will be better off as judged by themselves. In other words, boundedly rational agents should be subjected to paternalistic regulation. (The volume edited by McCaffery and Slemrod, 2006, is a useful collection of writings on behavioural public finance.)

5 Size of the public sector and costs of taxation to support that size

Historically, government spending relative to GDP has displayed an upward trend in most countries of the world. This was particularly prominent in the quarter century after 1950 when, following the lead of the UK, the model of the welfare state was adopted in one country after another. There was a reversal of the trend after the sweeping privatise–liberalise reforms of the 1980s. Since 2000, the ratio has picked up once again in the wake of 'bringing the state back in' response to the failure of those reforms to deliver adequately on their extravagant promises.

The up-down-up behaviour of government size over time has attracted the attention of researchers. The earliest observations in this field are captured in Wagner's law.

Wagner's law

In the second half of the nineteenth century, Adolph Wagner noted that in most countries of the world (his data covered a small set of industrialised countries), the size of the public sector tended to increase steadily over time. The exercise was repeated later for a larger set of nations with government expenditure/GDP as the measure of size and the same upward time trend were observed. This became known as Wagner's law.

For the USA, the ratio was 3.9 per cent in 1870 and 43 per cent in 2009; for the OECD, the average was 47 per cent in the same year. For Sweden, it peaked at 66 per cent in 1996 and declined thereafter. Currently, it is 18 per cent for India, 28.8 per cent for China and above

DOI: 10.4324/9781003585404-6

40 per cent for the USA, UK, Japan, France and Sweden. The size for the USA, the most private sector-friendly nation of the world, is noteworthy. The federal and state governments there are big purchasers of the private sector's output, with military purchase by the Department of Defence topping the list in value terms.

The reason commonly offered as an explanation of Wagner's law is that as GDP grows, the country requires more extensive and complex regulatory setups and the government takes public goods supply and its other social responsibilities (like the provision of social safety nets) more seriously. In the words of economic historian Douglass North, "There are no cases of complex high-income societies that do not have an elaborate structure of government".

Sceptics (and public choice theorists) will say that lobbying power of interest groups rises disproportionately with affluence, eliciting greater expenditure from the government on diverse fronts. This is particularly true in democratic countries where coalition politics rules. As supporting evidence, it may be noted that spikes in public expenditure are clearly discernible in the budgetary data of such countries just before important elections.

Even in the absence of pressure group politics, Wagner's law may be in operation because the people in government might seek revenue for their own personal benefits. Larger spending may be directed to increased salaries, better offices and more frequent and extensive travel or to other uses that promise to improve political support. Such self-serving behaviour would not be possible if taxpayers could control government decisions about public finances. Unfortunately, the lack of information and the unavailability to the citizens of effective instruments of punishment preclude such control. Accountability of government in fiscal matters remains fairly low, even in well-functioning democracies.

If size is measured by the labour force employed, the public sector's share remains fairly high, particularly in the developing countries, even after considerable downsizing after the economic reforms enforced by the WB and the IMF.

By now, it should not come as a surprise to the reader that there is a long-standing (and heated) debate about the appropriate size of the public sector vis-à-vis the private. The public choice school tirelessly repeats that almost all modern economies have public sectors of 'exaggerated size', but no guidelines are provided for the right size.

Public sector too small

Conservative economists love to claim that free market capitalism stands for democracy of the marketplace where dollar votes of consumers decide which goods will be produced and sold. But the analogy is flawed. While in the political sphere it is 'one man, one vote', in the marketplace richer persons have more dollar votes, imparting a bias in favour of goods and services consumed by the rich. Free market will devote resources mostly to the production of this set. One example is the coexistence of hungry children whose parents do not have sufficient purchasing power with grain-fed pigs and cows which provide meat for consumers with lots of purchasing power. State intervention is essential to correct the bias.

There is a more subtle factor to which economists and sociologists have drawn attention over the years. This is the phenomenon of *induced preference*, demand being promoted from the side of supply. Traditional welfare analysis, which shows that under certain conditions free market transactions achieve the social optimum, is based on the assumption of fixed, immutable preferences of consumers uninfluenced by any action on the part of the sellers. But induced wants are indubitably true, as even the most casual introspection reveals. Empirical support lies in the astronomical amounts spent every year by business on sales promotion.

As a society becomes affluent, wants begin to take on a relative nature. They expand keeping in pace with the increasing power to satisfy them. Massive sales promotion by business acts as a powerful engine behind this expansion. Consumers are caught like mice on a treadmill of ever-growing wants. Therefore, despite the enormous growth of productive capacity over the past century or more, citizens never feel inclined to reduce their purchasing power by paying taxes. This is reinforced by the traditional belief that governments are inherently inefficient and incapable of producing anything of value. The elastic nature of induced wants of the rich prompts many economists to assert that social welfare will be improved more by an expansion of government expenditure relative to private consumption expenditure. The earliest prominent advocate of this view is John Kenneth Galbraith, who, in his book *The Affluent Society*, first forcefully drew attention to the 'private splendour–public squalor' aspect of the American Society of the 1950s and 1960s. This, however, implicitly assumes that the government is better aware of the 'true' needs of the citizens, an assumption that has not gone unchallenged by the critics of big government.

Public sector too big

Critics of government point to the phenomenon of *logrolling* as a source of unnecessarily swollen government budgets. Logrolling in the public sector refers to a practice in which different organisations promote each other's agendas, each in the expectation that others will reciprocate. This features prominently in what in American usage is called pork barrel politics, in which logrolling is done to promote localised public projects that will boost the earnings of the political representatives of particular regions. This leads to wasteful proliferation of public projects. In developing countries, including India, numerous public sector projects are started in unsuitable areas just to generate votes for the locally elected politician who can pull strings at the top level.

The bureaucracy–business–politician nexus frequently induces the undertaking of needlessly big and/or socially unnecessary public projects. In Japan, they are called 'roads to nowhere', but they exist everywhere. There was a USD 400 million project to build a bridge to Gravina Island in Alaska to replace the ferry that was serving the fifty residents of that place. It was cancelled after national protests broke out, but $28 million had already been spent to build the approach roads. All over the developing world, examples are legion of such wasteful spending of public money that goes into the pockets of the politically connected. This is by no means absent in the rich countries (as the Alaska bridge case shows), though their effect is less crippling than in the poorer ones. When your budget is other people's money, it is extremely difficult not to be generous in your spending for your own benefit or that of your cronies. The bigger the budget, the larger the scope for such malfeasance. According to the conservatives, the only way the evil can be kept within tolerable limits is by keeping the government small.

No economist of either camp has succeeded in giving a formula for the right size of government. There is broad agreement though that there should be checks and balances to prevent both unbridled growth and excessive shrinkage of state activities. In democracies, the verdict of citizens in elections is the final arbiter. Unfortunately, there is a psychological stumbling block here. *Rational ignorance* may prevent voters from playing a socially useful role. Ignorance about an issue is called rational when the cost of acquiring and processing information about it can, in the agent's opinion, outweigh any potential benefit he or she hopes to gain by being educated about it. Since the details of budgetary policy (items of revenue or spending) are not easily or costlessly available, most voters may choose to remain uninformed on the costs and benefits. This will tend to produce an 'incorrect' budget in a democracy.

A big size of government goes hand in hand with high taxation to fund the spending. This imposes several costs on the economy. To that, we now turn.

Costs of taxation

Revenue is needed to supply public and merit goods and for transfers and subsidies as redistributive measures. The alternative to taxation is to borrow from the public or the central bank (the last option is available only to the central government). Borrowing from the central bank (called debt monetisation) is equivalent to adding to the domestic supply of money. Fiscal action backed by debt monetisation is actually a combination of fiscal and monetary actions.

Taxation, as we know, is of two types – direct and indirect. We take up indirect taxation first.

Cost of indirect taxation

Figure 5.1 shows the demand and supply curves for a particular commodity in a particular period. The free market solution is at point E, with price P_1 and total quantity transacted Q_1.

An indirect tax of Rs t per unit (AB) drives a wedge between the price paid by the buyer (the tax-inclusive price) and the price received by the seller net of tax. The difference is the tax collected per unit. As a result of the tax, the quantity bought and sold has fallen from Q_1 to Q_2. Total revenue collected is the area ABDC, equal to the per-unit tax AB times the tax base Q_2 (BD).

The inefficiency of the tax stems from the fact that Q_1 Q_2 amount of potential transactions mutually beneficial to both the buyer and the seller has been choked off. The triangular area CDE, called the *deadweight loss*, is the measure of this inefficiency. A higher tax rate will cause this loss to increase by further reducing the volume of transactions.

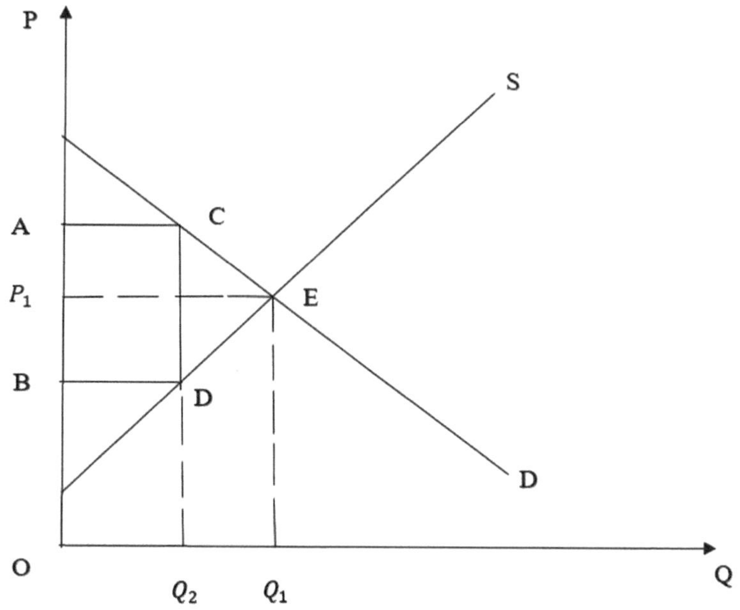

Figure 5.1 Cost of indirect tax.

Though precise estimates are not available, some studies for the USA suggest that one extra dollar of government tax revenue causes the loss of output also valued approximately one dollar. The implication is that the cost of one dollar of spending is actually two dollars (one dollar of tax plus one dollar of lost output).

An efficiency-equity conflict emerges in this context. Clearly, the deadweight loss will be lower than the reduction in quantity as a result of the tax. It should be clear from the figure that the fall in quantity will be lower if the demand curve is steeper. A steeper curve implies lower price elasticity of demand or lower responsiveness to price change.

Price elasticity of demand is likely to be low for goods and services that do not have close substitutes. They are necessities by nature, basic food, clothing, shelter and basic medicines being the prime examples. By our analysis, efficiency loss from taxation will be low for these items. But these are also the commodities that account for the highest share of the consumption budget of the poor. Higher taxation, recommended on efficiency grounds, will contradict the principle of social justice or equity.

This contradiction will be absent when tax is imposed on addictive goods like alcohol and tobacco, for which, because of addiction, substitution possibilities are low.

Land is a factor of production that cannot evade tax by moving to other locations. Its supply curve is vertical. Therefore, from the efficiency angle, a tax on its value or earnings (rent) may be highly desirable. In the second half of the nineteenth century, the American economist Henry George made this argument the basis for his radical single tax proposal – all taxes other than a land tax are to be done away with. Since the owners of land generally belong to the richer classes of society, the principle of equity will also be satisfied.

The tax, however, will not be harmless when it applies to improved land in which landlords have invested resources to improve its quality or build property on it. A land tax will damage efficiency by discouraging such expenditure.

Tariffs or import duties are an important source of revenue for many governments. They also have a strongly protective effect for domestic business. By raising the local price of importables, they weaken the blow of foreign competition. In some cases, this has indeed helped some infant industries to grow up and be globally competitive. The automobile and electronic goods industries of South Korea initially enjoying protection against Japanese imports provide the best-known examples. Unfortunately, in the majority of other cases, protection against foreign competition only encouraged inefficiency and indifference to product quality. The policy of 'infant industry protection' can at best show a mixed record of performance, with failures commanding a higher proportion.

One major pillar of the worldwide economic reforms programme of the 1990s was the lowering (with a view to ultimate abolition) of import duties and other barriers to free international trade in goods and services. The share of trade tax revenue in total tax revenue has come down substantially in India and other developing countries. Reduction in the cost of imported inputs has benefitted local companies, and at the same time, they have been compelled to pay more attention to efficiency improvements. Consumer welfare has gone up substantially due to greater attention to product quality.

Value-added tax

A VAT is an indirect tax that is paid on the value added at different stages of the production of a commodity. The chief advantage is the avoidance of multiple taxation and less evasion. Suppose VAT is 15 per cent and a person buys a piece of furniture for Rs 3000. Tax equals Rs 450 at this stage. The carpenter has paid Rs 1000 for the wood (an intermediate product) used to make the furniture and has paid a tax of Rs 150. When the furniture is sold, the seller pays Rs 300 (Rs 450 – Rs 150) to the government, after providing proof through receipts of the tax paid on purchasing the wood. By producing the furniture, the carpenter has added Rs 2000 to the value of the wood purchased (Rs 1000). He pays Rs 300, 15 per cent of Rs 2000, as tax. He receives a credit on tax paid on intermediate purchase.

A uniform sales tax of 15 per cent would be paid every time a market transaction took place in the chain of production stages, leading to what is known as tax escalation or cascading.

VAT has implications for tax compliance. Under it, buyers of intermediate products report their expenditures to tax administration to claim deductions against their own tax liabilities. This prevents sellers of the intermediates from not reporting or under-reporting their own sales revenues. This self-policing feature makes tax evasion difficult.

A large number of countries, including India, have adopted VAT or some modified version of it as the mode of indirect taxation. In recent years, India has taken a radical fiscal step by introducing the GST.

India's GST

The introduction of GST in July 2017 is a major change in the structure of India's indirect taxation. Previously, the union had the power to collect taxes on production, and the states could tax consumption. Only the union had the power to tax services. Following a constitutional amendment, central and state tax bases have been merged, and from this common base, the governments at both levels draw their revenues. This common base plus the input tax credit feature has eliminated a fragmented tax regime with its cascading effects and resulted in major procedural uniformity and simplification. The effect on trade, investment and business in general is expected to be beneficial.

The GST replaced the old central sales tax which was levied at the point of production. This was favourable for the producing states, but adversely affected the consuming states, who faced a higher price. This is why some richer producing states are still not very happy with the new system. But discontent has diminished over time as all states have come to enjoy the benefits due to revenue gain from base expansion and inclusion of services and an agreed formula that assigns a greater share to the states.

Since GST is an indirect tax unrelated to the purchasing power of the buyer, it is regressive in nature. Therefore, social justice requires a reduction in its importance as a source of revenue. Unfortunately, hardly any sign is discernible that GoI is seriously concerned about this issue. On the positive side, improved revenues have enabled higher spending on many projects and schemes that are of direct benefit to the poor. (For a discussion of various aspects of India's GST, see Chakraborty and Gupta.)

Cost of direct taxation

Increase in the rate of corporate taxation may discourage investment and risk-taking by business because of reduced after-tax returns. Property taxation may reduce the incentive to accumulate wealth by saving on the part of the rich. Liberal economists will be happy if the revenue collected from property taxation is used to subsidise the consumption of merit goods by the poor, to impart training to enhance their job prospects or to improve the economic condition of the backward regions of the country. All this, of course, presupposes a fair degree of honesty and sincerity on the part of the government officials.

Income taxation may have an adverse effect on the incentive to work. The resulting fall in labour supply may reduce the economy's actual output below its potential. The conservative economists attach great weight to this negative effect on growth. Before looking at the empirical evidence on this issue, we note that theoretically a change in income tax rates exerts two opposing effects on planned labour supply.

Lower income tax rates raise the taxpayer's base income, and at lower income levels, people may want to work less and enjoy more leisure. This is called the income effect which operates because at lower tax rates a given amount of work yields higher income. Pulling in the opposing direction in the substitution effect: higher after-tax returns to work make leisure less attractive and induce higher labour supply. The net effect of a lower income tax rate will depend on the relative strengths of the two opposing pulls. Labour supply will go up only if the substitution effect dominates the income effect. Applied to the case of higher tax rates, the lower returns to work will induce, on the one hand, greater work effort (less leisure) because taxpayers have less money to spend, but, on the other, make added effort less attractive by reducing the return. The conservatives think that the second factor (the substitution effect) will outweigh the first (the income effect). Empirical evidence for most of the advanced economies fails to support the view that labour supply is strongly affected by changes in income tax rates.

The possible disincentive effect on work effort is relevant for indirect taxation too. But here also the ultimate impact is indeterminate in principle. A general increase in consumer goods prices (because of higher sales or excise taxes) makes consumers with relatively fixed money incomes worse off, and this may induce more supply of labour. The rewards from more work have, however, gone down in terms of purchasing power, and this may discourage work. Empirical evidence here also is inconclusive.

House rents, interest payments on loans taken to purchase houses or consumer durables like cars and expenditure for children's education are some examples of committed expenditures that must be incurred by wage earners. Their levels cannot be adjusted downwards when income falls. Consumption spending, which is the main determinant of a family's standard of living, is supported by income in excess of these committed expenditures. The implication is that when these expenses figure prominently in a household's budget, higher income taxation may call for longer working hours (in the form of accepting or extending overtime work, entry of new family members into the labour force and so on) to maintain the family's living standards. Higher income tax rates, therefore, are more likely to induce more work effort by wage earners with a large number of dependents, particularly if they are in the process of setting up homes, bringing up children and running up debt to acquire consumer durables.

The administrative cost of collecting a given amount of revenue via direct taxation will be high in societies where tax evasion is high and/or corrupt officials manage to pass on less than the full amount collected to the public exchequer. This is a major reason why the developing countries have to resort to heavy indirect taxation for generating revenue. This is socially undesirable because of the regressive nature of sales or excise taxation. The burden is the same irrespective of the buyer's ability to pay.

More than 80 per cent of India's tax collections still come from indirect taxes. This indicates a major failure of the attempts to rationalise our tax system and to make it more fair.

Expenditure tax

One adverse effect of income tax that has received considerable attention is its effect on saving. Over the ages, a group of economists have criticised income taxation for its double penalty on saving. According to them, saving is taxed first as part of income and then again as the returns on invested saving become taxable. The result is a distortion in favour of consumption at the expense of thrift. They have recommended an *expenditure tax* or a *spending tax* as a better alternative.

In this alternative, the tax base is spending, not income. John Stuart Mill, a classical economist, wrote that the only "perfectly unexceptionable and just principle of income tax is to exempt all savings". Nicholas Kaldor, writing in 1955, persuasively argued that spending was a better measure of ability to pay than income. People should be taxed on what they take out of the common pool for their personal use, not on what they put into it. Additionally, income is deficient because it takes no account of differences among individuals as to the need to save.

There are two arguments against a spending tax: (a) administrative feasibility is low, and the specific provisions for taxpayer reporting are hard to formulate; (b) exemption of saving would favour the rich, who are better able to save. Advocates of spending tax have suggested ways of tackling (a) and have countered (b) by stating that the rate of tax may be made progressive in order to tax the rich as heavily as desired.

Though some of its advantages are recognised, considerable doubt persists about the administrative feasibility of expenditure taxation. Only two countries, India and Sri Lanka, have experimented with this type of tax in a limited form. By 1966, it was dropped by both.

The idea that high rate of income taxation may lead to a fall in production by inducing households to reduce labour supply has led conservative economists to make some fiscal recommendations.

Total tax revenue is the product of the tax rate and the tax base (value of income or GDP). Revenue will be low when the tax rate is low; it is also low when the tax rate is very high. The reason is that high rates may discourage people from work and output will fall as a result, bringing tax revenue down. Hence, the relationship between tax rate and tax revenue is expected to be hill shaped, first rising and then falling. This is known as the Laffer curve. In such a case, there will be tax rate that maximises revenue. If the actual rate is beyond this particular rate, moving to a lower one would actually raise both national income and tax revenue, and budget deficit will decline. Conservative economists tend to believe that this result is valid for Europe and the USA at present. But this claim has failed to obtain convincing support from empirical research.

The chief difficulty with the labour supply argument is that, as already noted, empirical evidence fails to support the hypothesis of a strong response of labour supply to changes in income taxation. It is also by no means easy to verify that a country's tax rate is really beyond the optimum that maximises tax collection.

It is, however, plausible that a higher tax rate may lead to higher tax evasion. This will affect tax revenue adversely.

Very costly state support – EU and India

Let us now turn to two notorious cases of very costly state support. These are in the form of subsidies (negative tax) to producers. From the point of view of efficiency, subsidies can be as harmful as taxes.

The European Union's Common Agricultural Policy

Despite its small share in GDP (around 2 per cent), agriculture in the developed countries is truly special in terms of its ability to influence government policy. The magnitude of state support extended to the farmers of these countries is astronomical. Just to give an idea, in 2004 farm support policies in the European Union (EU) amounted to $133 billion (33 per cent of farmers' income); in the USA, $38 billion (18 per cent); and in Japan, $49 billion (an amazing 56 per cent). Farmers producing rice, milk, sugar, wheat, beef, sheepmeat, corn and other grains are the biggest beneficiaries of these subsidies.

For the most part, the subsidy is provided through price supports which guarantee a minimum price to farmers. In the EU under the

Common Agricultural Policy (CAP), the extremely high levels of MSP have created extraordinary distortions. They have caused many farm products from being importable to being actually exported. Butter and other dairy products are prominent examples. With free trade, these products (and wheat for the UK and France) will be imported because the no-trade domestic prices are higher than the world prices. The support prices are so high that farmers produce much more than what the EU consumers would buy. A part of this excess production is exported with the help of export subsidies, and the rest is simply destroyed. So the situation is really strange. Price supports have morphed into a combination of import protection and export subsidies that are extremely lucrative for the farmers. And it is very costly for the EU, accounting for an average of nearly 50 per cent of total yearly fiscal expenditure. The loss inflicted on consumers has been estimated to amount to billions of euros per annum. Under intense pressure from other countries spanning over decades, the system has been changed to some extent from subsidy per unit to direct payment for production curbs that will keep the prices high but will not generate excess production.

There is a negative environmental side too to these subsidies. Most of these support meat and dairy farming which contribute heavily to greenhouse gas emissions and water and air pollution. Unfortunately, the lobbying power of big farmers has in recent years led to a watering down of Green European Union policy.

India's farm support programme

In India, farmers enjoy MSP for twenty-three mandated crops, including wheat and rice, in addition to being exempted from income tax. Prices of some fertilisers have been decontrolled, but heavy subsidy on nitrogen-based urea fertilisers continues. Excess production is bought up by the government at the MSP and stored in Food Corporation of India (FCI) godowns all over the land. Part of this stock is distributed to the poor through fair price shops, and the rest is held as reserves against unforeseen contingencies. The cost of running this programme is enormous. In addition, it is also unfair.

The benefits are enjoyed mostly by the big farmers of Punjab and Haryana. For the year 2021–2022, 97 per cent of the paddy produced was procured at MSP in Punjab. In contrast, procurement was quite low in the major paddy-producing states like West Bengal and Uttar

Pradesh. The number of big farmers being much lower in these two (and other) states, their lobbying power is also lower.

Although the support is for twenty-three crops officially, in practice it has come down to high procurement price, mainly for wheat and rice. This has made our agriculture dominated by these two crops. Actually, soil- and climate-wise, Punjab is not suited for rice production at all.

The heavy subsidy on nitrogen-based granular urea as fertiliser has led to an overuse of nitrogen (N) that has adverse consequences for soil fertility in the long run. Under strong criticism by agro-scientists, some limited movement has been initiated in recent years towards other types of fertilisers. There is vested interest against the switch, because a part of the subsidised material is diverted to non-agricultural uses and also smuggled out to neighbouring countries, where the price is higher.

Agricultural growth in India has failed to keep pace with that of industry and services. As a result, farm income is declining in relative terms. This has led to agitation, headed mostly by the big farmers, for a hefty upward revision of MSP for the major crops. The government has successfully resisted this to date and, in our judgement, should continue to do so. Further increases in MSP will lead to bigger surplus to be stored in FCI warehouses, where the existing stock is much more than that warranted by buffer norms.

The first best solution is to improve the productivity and competitiveness of agriculture, so that incomes can improve from domestic sales and exports can go up. Export expansion is hindered by the high protection currently afforded to agriculture in the developed countries. The fight against this blatant protectionism in international trade negotiations must continue. Public investment in agricultural infrastructure in India has slowed down steadily over time because of the ever-rising expenditure on price support and input subsidy. One can hardly expect a long-term improvement in productivity in this scenario. (Jana and Mondal in Chatterjee and Sasmal, 2024, contains an overview of farm subsidy and other aspects of Indian agriculture.)

Tax evasion and the shadow economy

When payment of income and other direct taxes is based on self-reporting, a section of the population may choose to under-report. As a deterrent, governments have the policy of random auditing (because auditing every tax return is prohibitively costly) plus punishment in case under-reporting is detected. Random audit introduces a probability of detection in the calculations of potential evaders. But raising the detection probability is costly because of additional personnel required for auditing. Increasing the penalty in the form of fines does not have any associated cost.

Evasion is not confined to direct taxes alone. Indirect taxes, like sales taxes or import duties, are evaded when goods are smuggled across borders from low-tax areas. Multinational corporations with operations in different countries with different tax structures can adopt clever strategies, known as *transfer pricing,* to shift profits from high-tax to low-tax locations by manipulating the values of intra-firm transactions. This way of reducing total tax liability may be considered a form of international smuggling.

In the shadow (or black) economy, incomes are not reported to the authorities at all. The informal sector in India and other developing countries where a high proportion of the labour force works is a prominent example of such an economy. Its existence is by no means negligible for the developed nations.

Since the size of the shadow economy cannot be directly observed, various indirect methods of estimation have been tried. According to some estimates, the size of the shadow economy as a proportion of GDP is 30 per cent or more for some countries like Italy, the UK, Spain, Greece and Portugal. There is evidence that this ratio is getting bigger over time everywhere in the world.

The shadow economy (tax evasion in general) may be expected to be larger where social norms are more tolerant of dishonesty and where people do not have trust in their government to spend tax revenue in socially beneficial ways. (Chattopadhyay, 2018, and Kumar, 2017, are good introductions to economists' approach to black markets and black money.)

6 Fiscal policy in global context

So far, our discussion has been restricted to the domestic economy in isolation from the world. We now proceed to put fiscal action in an international context. This is important because over the last four decades or so most countries have gradually become more and more integrated with the rest of the world. This is particularly true of the developing countries in the post-reform scenario. They are collectively known as the emerging market economies.

The openness to the world at large covers openness in both current and capital accounts.

The current account of a nation's balance of payments (BoP) records the export and import of currently produced goods and services. A more open current account means fewer restrictions on international trade. The major restrictions are import or export taxes and quantitative restrictions such as import quotas. A country's trade balance is positive when the value of exports exceeds the value of imports.

The capital account of BoP records transactions in financial assets across national borders. When an Indian citizen buys stocks (equity) or bonds sold by foreign nationals, it is the capital outflow from India; when a foreign national buys Indian financial assets, it is the capital inflow into India.

Among the major types of capital flows, foreign direct investment (FDI) is long term (more than one year) and consists of equity purchases amounting to at least ten per cent of the value of the firm, whereas foreign portfolio investment (FPI) is typically short-term transactions in bonds or equity. The chief distinguishing feature is that FPI flows change directions quickly prompted by prospects of capital

DOI: 10.4324/9781003585404-7

gains, while FDI is driven by long-term profitability considerations. The latter is far less volatile than the former. Global capital flows today are predominantly short-term FPI flows.

Restrictions on movement of funds in and out of a country for asset transactions are known as *capital controls*. Liberalisation of foreign trade involves the removal of both current account trade barriers and of capital controls. Since the economic reforms of the early 1990s, India has moved much further in the direction of greater openness in current account than in capital.

The exchange rate between currencies plays a very important role in open economies. Let's briefly discuss how its value gets determined.

We assume for simplicity that India and the USA are the only two countries engaged in trade. An Indian needs dollars for two purposes: (i) when he wants to import (say) personal computers from the USA and (ii) when he wants to buy shares or bonds issued by an American company. Denoting the values of imports and capital outflows by M and CO, respectively, the value of total dollar demand can be represented as (M + CO). On the other side, an American will need rupees for two purposes: (i) to import (say) shirts from India (India's current account export) and (ii) to buy Indian financial assets. The American national will have to sell dollars in the foreign exchange market to obtain Indian rupees. This stands for dollar supply. Denoting the values of India's exports and capital inflows by X and CI, respectively, the value of total dollar supplied is (X + CI).

The foreign exchange market will be in balance (equilibrium) when total demand for dollar is equal to total supply. The condition can be written as

$$X + CI = M + CO \tag{6.1}$$

It should be noted that in Equation 6.1, we are considering private dollar flows only. If there are official transactions (usually by a central bank), the relation will have to be modified to

$$X + CI = M + CO + RC \tag{6.2}$$

RC stands for change in foreign exchange reserve of the central bank. RC is positive (negative) when the central bank buys (sells) foreign exchange, which is dollar in our case.

Determination of the exchange rate

The rupee–dollar exchange rate is defined to be the ratio (rupee/dollar) – how much rupee is to be given up to buy one dollar. In other words, it is the price of dollar (in units of rupee) in the foreign exchange market. An increase in the exchange rate (rise in the price of dollar) is depreciation of rupee, whereas a decrease in the exchange rate is rupee appreciation. Depreciation discourages imports by raising the rupee price of imports and stimulates exports by lowering the dollar price of exports.

Exchange rate systems

a Flexible or floating exchange
Here, the exchange rate (the price of dollar in our analysis) is determined by the forces of demand and supply in the market for foreign exchange. The government or the central bank (Reserve Bank of India in our case) does not intervene. The value of the exchange rate will settle at a level, the market clearing level or equilibrium level, where dollar demand and supply (the two sides of Equation 6.1) are equal. At a higher rate, supply will exceed demand, and at a lower rate, demand will be greater than supply.

Anything that changes the demand or supply of dollars (driven by changes in the underlying factors, X, M, CI or CO) will cause the exchange rate to change.

An increase in the US demand for made-in-India products will increase the demand for rupees and the supply of dollars. It will cause the market clearing value of the exchange rate to decrease, a rupee appreciation. If foreign investors want to buy more shares in Indian blue-chip companies (higher FPI) or expand production or marketing facilities in India (higher FDI), the effect will be the same. If investors want to move their funds out of India, the result is an increase in CO. Rupee assets will be sold to demand more dollars to purchase more American assets. Under flexible exchange, the exchange rate (price of dollar) will rise, a rupee depreciation.

Fixed exchange system

Under flexible exchange, the central bank does nothing to influence the exchange rate. On the other hand, in a fixed exchange system, the central bank fixes the value of the rupee–dollar rate. It is price control imposed in the market for foreign exchange. Since the fixed price will generally be different from the market clearing price, there must be official intervention to support it. The central bank must stand ready to buy or sell currencies at the announced fixed rate.

If the announced rate is higher than the equilibrium rate, supply of dollar will exceed demand for it. Unless the excess supply is removed from the market, it will exert a downward pressure on the exchange rate. To prevent this, the central bank will have to buy dollars in the required amount in exchange for rupees. The stock of foreign reserves will go up. RC will be positive in Equation 6.2. Conversely, if the official rate is below the equilibrium value, dollar demand will be greater than supply and the central bank will have to supply the appropriate amount from its dollar stock to support the announced rate. Foreign reserves will fall, and RC will be negative.

Completely flexible or fixed exchange rates are two extreme regimes. Most countries today, including India, follow a middle path of managed exchange, where there is intervention to keep fluctuations in the rate under control. Variations within a band are tolerated.

A natural question to ask at this point is why should the central bank intervene in the foreign exchange market at all. The answer is that too much fluctuation in such an important variable as the exchange rate is undesirable. Fund flows in today's global finance are heavily dominated by short-term FPI, which are very volatile in nature, because they are driven by the prospect of making quick capital gains. They are very unpredictable, unlike long-term FDI flows. Sudden and large changes in CI or CO will cause the exchange rate in a flexible system to experience large unforeseen swings over short periods. This may be very damaging for those engaged in current or capital account transactions.

Foreign exchange intervention has monetary consequences. When the central bank sells dollar at the fixed rate in exchange for rupees, domestic money supply falls as rupee is withdrawn from circulation. Conversely, when the bank buys dollars and pays rupees in exchange, money supply (liquidity) goes up as this newly created rupee was not in circulation before. This link between the foreign exchange market and domestic liquidity via central bank operations is absent when the system is one of fully flexible exchange.

Economic policies under different exchange regimes

Under fixed exchange system, the central bank has to purchase or sell dollar as conditions change to defend the value of the exchange rate.

This will lead to changes in domestic supply of money. For example, suppose there is a movement away from Indian assets so that CO goes up. This will create pressure for the rupee to depreciate. This pressure must be offset to maintain the exchange rate at its announced level. The central bank will sell dollar (purchase rupee). Domestic money supply will shrink in the process. The opposite will happen in situations where pressure emerges for rupee appreciation.

The lesson is that the task of maintaining a stable value of the exchange rate deprives the central bank of its control over money supply. Monetary policy is lost as an instrument. The loss will be partial if the exchange rate is allowed to vary within a band, rather than being absolutely fixed. Monetary policy retains its power under flexible exchange.

What happens when fiscal expansion (higher public spending, lower taxation or both) is undertaken under flexible exchange? With no change in money supply, such expansion will (i) raise the demand for imports by stimulating home income and (ii) push up the home interest rate as the government borrows more to finance its spending. Interest rate is the return on home bonds. The return on domestic equity will also increase as all asset returns tend to move together. This increase in the return on home bond and equity will attract larger capital inflow from abroad.

What happens to the exchange rate is ambiguous. The rise in imports raises the demand for dollars, while larger CI will raise its supply. The net effect depends crucially on the responsiveness of fund flows to increase in asset returns. If this responsiveness (also known as the *degree of capital mobility*) is high, the boost in dollar supply will be larger than that in demand and rupee will appreciate (dollar will depreciate, which is the same thing from the other side). This, however, will tend to lower NX by raising imports and depressing exports. Because NX is part of AD, this will partly offset the stimulating effect of the initial fiscal boost on GDP. The effectiveness of fiscal action is lowered. Some economists call this 'crowding out through exchange rate', to contrast with crowding out in a closed economy which operates solely via an increase in the interest rate.

It is easy to check that when the degree of capital mobility is low, dollar demand will go up following a fiscal expansion, and rupee will depreciate. This depreciation will boost GDP on its own by raising NX.

Thus, under flexible exchange, fiscal action becomes more effective if the degree of capital mobility is lower.

What happens under fixed exchange? With high mobility of funds, fiscal expansion creates pressure for rupee appreciation. To keep the exchange rate fixed, this pressure has to be neutralised. The central bank will buy dollar and sell rupee, thereby raising the money supply. This will reduce the force of domestic crowding out by moderating the upward pressure on interest rates. Fiscal action becomes more effective in raising GDP. The opposite happens if the degree of mobility is low.

Under the sweeping liberalisation programme of economic reforms, a worldwide movement is towards more flexible exchange rate and higher fund mobility (through the removal of capital controls). This combination is not welcome news for the supporters of fiscal action. It is to be noted in this context that both India and China have successfully resisted pressure to remove capital controls completely. Thanks to this plus better supervision of the domestic financial sector, they have been able to build up effective insulation against financial crises originating in volatile fund flows and their misuse by domestic banks. Because of much lower capital controls, Latin American countries have suffered much more from frequent bouts of financial crises, with devastating results for the domestic economy. This is the major reason why some pro-globalisation economists, such as Jagdish Bhagwati, are in favour of a policy mix that boosts the openness in current account transactions while maintaining strict supervision over cross-border financial flows. Both China and India have persistently defied the IMF to retain capital controls and have enjoyed greater gained insulation against shocks originating in foreign financial markets.

The policy of greater global integration calls for drastic elimination of or significant reduction in taxes on international trade. This has caused serious fiscal stress, because trade taxes used to constitute a high proportion of tax revenue of the developing countries. Since exports and imports are done by a relatively small number of agents, collection cost is much lower compared with other types of taxes. This explains the popularity of trade taxes. To reduce budget deficit in the wake of falling revenues, many governments have been forced to cut back on public expenditure. Since subsidies to big producers could not be cut due to their economic clout, in many instances the axe has fallen on public projects targeting the poor.

Taxation as capital control device

Capricious movement of financial funds, especially FPI, in and out of countries in response to changes in short-term returns coupled with the misuse of foreign borrowing by domestic banks and investors have been identified as major factors behind financial crises. Sudden stops in capital inflows or their reversal can lead to severe financial stress, creating deep recessions and forcing nations to default on foreign financial obligations. Prominent examples include Argentina (1995, 2002), Brazil (1998–1999) and Mexico (1994–1995). Impediments to free flow of funds may act as preventive device.

One such impediment is a tax that must be paid to the government equal to some percentage of foreign borrowing or a requirement that some portion of the borrowing or portfolio investment be placed in a zero-interest deposit with the country's central bank for a specified period. These restrictive measures may be useful in several ways. They can (a) discourage destabilising short-term flows and (b) reduce the country's exposure to contagion by limiting the amount that foreign lenders could pull out of the country at short notice.

Chile used these types of capital controls successfully during the 1990s. But many economists consider them as the second best policy. It is better if governments can identify the specific vulnerabilities that might lead to a crisis and address these directly. For example, if it is noticed that banks are using borrowed foreign funds to lend to non-viable private projects, the first best intervention is to improve financial regulation and bank supervision.

Also, capital controls are likely to lose their effectiveness over time as investors and borrowers find ingenious ways to circumvent them.

Fiscal policy in the European Union

The Maastricht Treaty formed the foundation for the EU, a collection of European countries, that decided to replace national currencies by the euro in 2002. Two fiscal criteria were included in a set of five that all members, actual or prospective, had to meet. These are as follows: (a) budget deficit must not exceed 3 per cent of GDP and (b) government debt must not be larger than 60 per cent of GDP. Temporary exceptions are allowed for exceptional circumstances only. Violation would attract monetary fines. These two conditions combined were known as the Stability and Growth Pact.

To take care of uniform monetary policy, the European Central Bank (ECB) was established as the centre of a federal structure that included national central banks as operating arms. Price stability was considered the prime target of coordinated monetary action.

With monetary union, each country gives up the freedom to take independent monetary action. Exchange rate adjustment is also lost as a tool because of the common currency. So, the entire burden of tackling domestic imbalances falls on fiscal policy. However, there is no blueprint for concerted fiscal action to fight business cycles in member countries. For example, higher tax revenue from the growing countries is not automatically transferred to recession countries in need of lower taxes and higher spending as stimulus.

In the early 2000s, the fiscal situation deteriorated in several European countries including France and Germany as slow growth led to low tax revenue. Budget deficits moved above the stipulated 3 per cent and persisted for several years. Sensibly enough, there was no attempt to raise taxes or cut spending. The union decided not to impose fines. In 2005, the Pact was broadened to recognise a larger set of exceptions.

One major problem with maintaining fixed exchange rates (not necessarily a monetary union) in general is that uncoordinated fiscal action may lead to large capital inflows or outflows. For instance, a big reduction by one country in taxes on financial investments may induce a big boost in capital inflows into that country. Foreign currency reserves will decline in other countries, as they try to defend their currencies against large-scale capital outflows. The resulting contractions in domestic money supply may trigger recessions.

Economies that are heavily dependent on the export of natural resources like petroleum, natural gas, copper, lithium and other metals and minerals may be subject to fiscal instability arising from global price fluctuations. Government budgets in these countries tend to become strongly linked to export earnings, so that an unforeseen drop in price forces cutbacks in public spending. Some countries, like Norway, have found a solution in the creation of the Sovereign Wealth Fund, which is a state-managed investment fund containing the revenue from natural resource exports. Oil was discovered off the coast of Norway in the 1970s. The sovereign fund was set up in 1990. Part of the earnings from oil exports goes into it every year. The Treasury uses a fraction of the investment returns for fiscal purposes, but the fund remains untouched.

7 Closer look at public debt

Control of public debt is the centrepiece of macroeconomic policies in most countries of the world today. Because it adds to existing debt, governments are not supposed to raise budget deficit even to fight recessions. Effectively, discretionary fiscal action has been taken out of the armoury of government policy tools.

Why is public debt and its growth viewed with so much alarm in mainstream economic thinking? The following discussion will examine its logic. Some of these points have already been touched in other chapters.

Change in the public debt equals current budget deficit, which is the excess of government spending over taxes. But one component of spending is interest payments on the existing debt. Total budget deficit may be written as the sum of PD (non-interest) plus interest payment on public debt. Changes in fiscal policy impact the PD. In the current period, governments cannot do anything about the debt they have inherited from the past. This has one important implication. The larger the debt, the higher will be the required interest payments, other things remaining the same. The funds used for this purpose cannot be used for promoting health, education, social safety nets or other desirable governmental activities. This gives us a good reason to be careful about the size of the national debt and the annual budget deficit that makes it grow.

Not only the size but the ownership of public debt also matters. Broadly speaking, the national debt is owned by three groups: the domestic public (both as individuals and through financial institutions), foreign investors and the domestic and foreign central banks.

DOI: 10.4324/9781003585404-8

The part that is domestically owned (which is about 70 per cent for India) can be thought of as a debt that we 'owe to ourselves'. The government using tax revenue to service this debt (paying interest and paying back the principal on maturity) may be considered costless because it is like taking money from the left pocket and putting it into the right. Not exactly though, because taxation for today's debt servicing is usually extended to future periods or generations. So, a question of intertemporal (intergenerational) equity arises. Why should future citizens or our future selves pay for government spending today?

The answer is that if government expenditure adds to social infrastructure and the supply of useful public goods (capital expenditure), the benefits will continue to flow over time. Future generations (or our future selves) will be better off as a result. Better infrastructure, at the same time, will enhance the ability to pay by boosting the growth of GDP. So, there is nothing unfair in asking future generations to bear part of the current cost. This argument loses validity if current borrowing is frittered away by the government in socially unproductive uses.

The part that is owned by foreigners cannot be treated as transfer from one pocket to another of the same person. An additional danger is that foreign lenders often insist on payment in foreign currency, usually (US) dollar. Three sources of obtaining dollar are export earnings, foreign capital inflow and converting tax revenue into dollar. If for some reason the first two flows shrink or tend to dry up, debt servicing will be a serious problem. Sensing trouble, foreign investors may want to pull their money back by selling off local financial assets or not renewing short-term loans. This will deepen the crisis. When foreign capital flows out on a big scale, the local currency undergoes depreciation (in a flexible exchange regime) and the same amount of government revenue collected in local currency will not be sufficient to service the fixed dollar obligations. Government funds may have to be diverted from other socially beneficial uses. This is a serious risk associated with foreign ownership of national debt.

When creditors become worried about a nation's ability to service its debt, they refuse to extend further credit or raise the interest rates on new loans. That, of course, makes it harder to service debt. Greece in the years following the GFC of 2007–2009 provides a classic case study.

Greece's sustained fiscal indiscipline played a key role in triggering the Eurozone debt crisis of the first decade of this century. It all began when in 2009 the newly elected Greek government candidly announced that the actual FD stood at 12.7 per cent of GDP, more than double the number announced by the previous government. In 2009, the country's debt-to-GDP ratio was 128 per cent. Over the next two years, as Greece's global credit rating nosedived, the interest rate it faced rose from 5.2 per cent to 15.7 per cent. The increased interest payment amounted to 13 per cent of GDP.

Investors began to worry seriously that sovereign default will occur soon, and their fear spread to cover other countries like Ireland, Italy, Portugal and Spain, all of which had been adversely affected by the collapse of domestic housing markets following the US example. World stock markets plunged as the prospect of a wider financial crisis grew. The value of the euro fell sharply in foreign exchange markets. The Greek government announced harsh budget cuts and raised taxes, but had to partially roll these back in the face of widespread street protests and strikes.

Total collapse could be averted when, in April 2010, Eurozone countries and the IMF agreed on a Euro 110 billion loan package for Greece.

A 'diabolical loop' often develops between public debt and financial health of banks. Weak governments (high perceived risk of sovereign default due to high FD) weaken banks that hold government bonds in their portfolio; weakened banks need more capital infusion, which often comes from public funds, weakening government finances further.

A striking illustration is provided by Ireland's experience in 2010. When government debt surged to 100 per cent of GDP, public expenditure was cut across a wide front. Unemployment rose sharply as a result. The debt explosion had occurred when the Irish government assumed the debt of its private banking sector after the bursting of the housing bubble in 2008. Interestingly, the reason behind the financial crisis was the corrupt behaviour of the same set of private banks, government officials and cronies in the construction industry.

Box 7.1 Twin Mexican debt crises

The first Mexican debt crisis erupted in 1982. In the preceding decade, public debt had increased from $4 billion to over $40 billion. Interest was to be paid in dollar, euro and pound. In

1981, inflation surged to 100 per cent and the Central Bank of Mexico decided to let the peso depreciate by 40 per cent against dollar. Wages increased to keep pace with inflation. In 1982, many private firms defaulted on their foreign debt, which had suddenly become 40 per cent higher in peso terms. Seized by panic, foreign funds left the country's financial system in huge amounts. The economy was in the grip of a severe crisis.

Debt restructuring and loans from the USA, the IMF and European commercial banks saved the situation. But the conditionalities imposed by the IMF (the SAP) extracted an enormous toll. Government spending was cut back, wage increases frozen, and interest rates were pushed up to very high levels in an attempt to reverse capital outflow. GDP fell by 10 per cent over two years, while unemployment and poverty increased significantly.

Mexico faced another severe crisis in the mid-1990s. IMF-mandated deregulation of the financial sector had encouraged domestic banks to borrow from foreign sources (mostly American) in order to lend to customers in Mexico. Domestic demand for loans was increasing because business wanted to expand operations in the growing economy. Growth prospects looked bright after the signing of the North American Free Trade Agreement (NAFTA) between Canada, the USA and Mexico.

However, after decades of tight regulation, banks were unprepared to give loans in large amounts. Due to mismanagement of borrowed funds or plain corruption on the part of the borrowers, many of these loans soon turned out to be bad. On top of this came the sharp devaluation of the peso vis-à-vis the US dollar at the end of 1994. Foreign liabilities of banks suddenly almost doubled in peso terms. With their balance sheets devastated, financial institutions stopped lending altogether and the economy went into a tailspin, with GDP falling by as much as 10 per cent in 1995. On the advice of the IMF, the Mexican government bailed out banks by buying their foreign debt. Thus, a major part of private foreign debt got transformed into public foreign debt.

India's debt-to-GDP ratio came down from 74.5 per cent in 2008 to 65.3 per cent in 2014. Since then, the average has stabilised between 70 and 80 per cent. More importantly, the external component denominated in foreign currency is low. The country has never come even close to default on its financial obligations. Actually, India, very conspicuously among the developing countries, has reputation for repaying foreign loans on time.

Is growth adversely affected by a high debt-to-GDP ratio? Although some economists claimed to have discovered a tipping point of 90 per cent beyond which higher debt is associated with growth shrinkage, this has not found support in more careful later research.

We can summarise by saying that the potential danger from accumulating public debt will be low if

i The external component (carrying payment obligations in foreign currencies) is low.
ii GDP growth is high leading to growth in tax collection. A useful condition, called the Domar condition, says that debt can be sustained over time if the growth rate of national income is not lower than the interest rate to be paid on government bonds. Too much reliance on this simple formula is, however, unwarranted.

Depending on the expectation of future growth rates and interest rates and other factors, one country's high debt-to-GDP ratio may be sustainable, while another's low ratio is not. Japan, with its average debt-to-GDP ratio exceeding 100 per cent, is yet to face any crisis, whereas Argentina with its much lower value is not trusted by international lenders and has to pay a much higher risk premium on its borrowing. The major part of Japanese debt is domestically owned.

India at present successfully meets both the conditions. But eternal vigilance is necessary to ensure that they continue to be met.

To keep the size of public debt under control, several countries have gone for debt ceiling laws. Only the USA and Denmark have set an upper limit in absolute amount, while for the EU it is 60 per cent of GDP. The legal cap on borrowing is de facto not binding for the US because it is invariably raised before the actual level gets that high. The current debt-to-GDP ratio is above 60 per cent. The ceiling has been raised under presidents Reagan, Bush (senior), Clinton and Obama. In

2023, President Biden signed the Fiscal Responsibility Act into law and the ceiling has been suspended till 2025. Many economists and policymakers are in favour of abolishing the debt ceiling altogether.

Debt–taxation equivalence

Some economists (see Barro, 1974) maintain that there is no fundamental difference between debt and taxation as a means of financing state expenditure. No government can go on running deficit indefinitely and hence will have to balance its budget in the long run, implying that a higher deficit caused by a tax cut today must be balanced by tax hikes at some point or points in the future, assuming no change in future government spending. Farsighted rational agents, it is claimed, will recognise that debt is nothing but deferred taxation. In order to shield themselves against future declines in consumption, they will raise their saving today. Higher public dis-saving (higher deficit) will be exactly matched by higher private saving, and aggregate saving in the economy will remain unchanged. A corollary follows. Since it will be entirely saved, current tax cut will not act as a fiscal stimulus, contrary to the claims of the Keynesians.

The validity of this proposition depends critically on a number of very unrealistic assumptions. In particular, it assumes that households are extremely farsighted, and they can borrow or lend in perfect capital markets. It can be shown that if agents are myopic (boundedly rational) and/or they face borrowing constraints in the current period, private consumption will indeed go up after a tax cut, as predicted by the Keynesian short-run consumption function. Empirical research has also contradicted the proposition. Tax cuts in the USA, Europe and elsewhere in recessions have indeed induced people to spend more.

Monetised debt, deficit and inflation

Central banks of all nations hold a part of public debt in the form of cumulative market purchase of government bonds over the years. This is essentially an interest-free loan, because the entire interest amount earned by the bank is returned to the government at the end of the financial year. So, apparently, the best option for the government is to sell all the debt to the central bank. But that may be costly, because central bank's purchase of assets adds to the supply of money in the economy. Doing this in excessive amounts will lead to inflation.

Financing debt by selling bonds to the central bank is known as 'debt monetisation'.

Hyperinflation is a situation of extremely high inflation. A working definition is a price rise of 1000 per cent per annum. Hyperinflation has occurred in Germany and Hungary during the 1920s and in Argentina, Bolivia, Brazil and Zimbabwe among other countries in more recent decades. In almost every case, the root cause can be diagnosed as extremely high growth of money supply. Unable to raise funds by any other means, governments financed skyrocketing expenditure by approaching the central banks for credit, which was provided by printing more money. Hyperinflation is debt monetisation running amok. Milton Friedman once famously said that "Inflation is always and everywhere a monetary phenomenon", which is true because sustained inflation is not possible without sustained rise in money supply. However, most of the time, the rise in money supply is driven by sustained debt monetisation. In this sense, hyperinflation is ultimately a fiscal phenomenon. This is another good reason for keeping a close watch on the magnitude of budget deficit and its source of financing.

Financial sector reform in India put a cap on the amount that GoI can annually borrow from the RBI. The objective is to keep debt monetisation within strict limits.

Inflation is unambiguously bad for the citizens (especially for those whose income is fixed in money terms), but for governments it may act as a potent instrument for drawing resources away from private use. This route of revenue extraction via price rise is known as *inflation tax* or *seigniorage*. It is based on the government's exclusive power to print money (via borrowing from the central bank) that can be used to purchase goods and services from the market.

An example may clarify. Suppose currently 100 units of output are being produced and price P = Rs 2 per unit and household's income equals Rs 200, just sufficient to purchase 100 units. Now, the government wants to take for its own use 10 units of output. It can do so in two ways: (i) raise Rs 20 in tax and buy 10 units at the going price and (ii) raise the money supply to push P up to such an extent that with its income of Rs 200, households (there is no explicit tax now) can buy only 90 units. The government is able to collect 10 units without imposing taxes, simply by debasing the currency through inflation. Understandably, it is a popular method in countries which do not have the ability or political will to collect direct taxes.

The purchasing power of extra money created is given by the formula:

Seigniorage = (growth rate of money supply) × (stock of real balances held by the public)

Real balance is money supply deflated by the aggregate price level.

In India, the inflation tax has never been a major source of tax revenue. The proportion of total revenue extracted via inflation is on average much higher for Latin America and Africa.

Financial repression provides revenue to the government by keeping the domestic interest rate artificially low and by restricting the rights of citizens to take their savings abroad. The interest rate available to investors in the global market may be 6 per cent, but the government may fix the domestic rate at 2 per cent to keep its own borrowing cost low. Control over funds outflow is necessary, because without it nobody will lend to the government at the low rate. Another method of financial repression was practised in India in the pre-reform era. Commercial banks were mandated to hold a certain (minimum) percentage set by the government (known as the Statutory Liquidity Ratio) of their portfolio in the form of low-yielding government bonds. Even after economic reforms, which lowered the Statutory liquidity ratio (SLR) substantially, Indian banks continue to hold government securities, but that is because such securities carry very low risk compared to private financial assets.

Just as budget deficits may create inflationary pressures by raising the supply of money, higher inflation can lead to larger budget deficits. There are two channels: tax collection effect and higher interest cost.

Taxes are paid on last year's nominal income. If in the meantime prices have gone up, the real value of tax revenue will be lower. Measured deficit includes interest payment on the national debt. Nominal interest rates go up in periods of rising prices, as lenders want to protect their return in real terms. Interest payments on debt increase as a result, pulling up the measured budget deficit in the process. To adjust for this effect, high-inflation countries calculate the inflation-adjusted deficit given by

Inflation-adjusted deficit = total deficit – (inflation rate) × national debt

We end this chapter by making an important observation. The vast majority of financial crises over the past half-century have had their origin in incorrect monetary policy and faulty regulation of private financial institutions. The incidence of debt crisis driven by fiscal indiscipline is much rarer in comparison. Perhaps the most desirable way to lowering the need for debt financing (and improving equity in distribution in the process) would be progressive taxation of income and wealth. But most governments, in developing and developed countries alike, are unwilling and /or unable to do this. And the official global agencies never put pressure on them to do so.

8 Government actions for sustainable long-term growth

The years 1980–2007 came to be known as the Great Moderation as economic fluctuations were relatively mild and the twin evils of unemployment and inflation were under control. With business cycles apparently tamed and Keynes consigned to the history of economic thought, mainstream economists, mainly in the USA, wanted full focus on long-term supply-side measures. Demand management by the government was considered an obsolete, misguided ritual of the past. Forget the economy, just manage the budget – was the confident admonition.

Onto this relative calm, the GFC (or the Great Recession) burst like a veritable tsunami in 2007. There was real concern that there will be total collapse like that of the Great Depression of the1930s. That, fortunately, could be prevented by prompt and concerted work by the Federal Reserve and other major central banks of the world, combined with carefully coordinated fiscal action on many fronts.

Clearly, the announcement of the death of Keynes and his fiscal activism by the conservatives was premature. Large-scale fiscal stimulus was undertaken in country after country to shore up aggregate expenditure and business confidence. And it worked. Inevitably, public debt soared to unprecedented heights and still remains high in most countries despite efforts over the past decade and a half to return to normal fiscal scenario. It has been emphatically demonstrated once again that concentration on the supply side alone will not ensure trouble-free growth.

(Barwell, 2016, contains a good review of the impact of the GFC on economic policy, monetary and fiscal.)

DOI: 10.4324/9781003585404-9

In 2000, the American Economic Association conducted a survey of 298 members. It was found that while 84 per cent agreed with the statement, 'Fiscal policy has a significant stimulative impact on a less than fully employed economy', 71 per cent also generally agreed with, 'Management of the1 business cycle should be left to the Federal Reserve, and activist fiscal policy should be avoided'. In 2011, a follow-up survey of 568 members showed that the previous majority acceptance of the second proposition has been replaced by a roughly 50:50 divide.

However, sustainable growth that a society should strive for encompasses much more than stabilisation against recessions, big or small, and even more than stable progress in conventionally measured GDP with price stability. We shall focus on two major aspects of sustainability over the long run – growth or development must be (i) inclusive and (ii) environmentally acceptable.

Economic development is inclusive if the fruits of growth are fairly shared. This calls for a reduction in both poverty and inequality. In 2000, the international community agreed upon a set of Millennium Development Goals (MDGs). The first one of a long list targeted a 50 per cent reduction by 2015 in the number of poor people from its level in 1990. (The poverty line was fixed at $1.25 a day or approximately $500 a year.) Happily, the target was met in 2010, due chiefly to poverty alleviation in India and China, the two countries accounting for a high proportion of global poverty. Government action played a major role. However, the absolute number of poor people in the world remains staggering. And poverty should not be restricted to income poverty alone. Poverty alleviation in its broadest sense should expand the capability set of the less privileged by improving health, nutrition, effective education, access to information and to public goods and greater participation in the community's decision-making. The good work of national governments with help from international institutions and non-governmental organisations (NGOs) must continue with renewed vigour.

Unregulated markets cannot be expected to keep distributional inequality in check, and they haven't done so. Global inequality was high and rising over 1870–1914, decreased noticeably in the post-Second World War era thanks in large part to the welfare state, but has been steadily on the rise since the 1980s. According to one estimate, the average income of the richest twenty nations was 16 times that of the poorest twenty in 1960; four decades later, the ratio was 35. At the same time, intra-country income gap and wealth gap are also growing. An emerging global elite, mostly urban based and interconnected in a variety of ways, is amassing great wealth and power, while over half of humanity is left to fend for itself against heavy odds.

As a manifestation of injustice, inequality is intrinsically undesirable. But it has negative implications even for efficiency. Inequality breeds conflict and encourages corruption and crimes. Crime control eats up valuable resources, and erosion of social cohesion may create a climate that is not conducive for private investment. Since the poor have a higher propensity to spend, high or rising inequality may act as a brake on growth by lowering the growth of demand for current production. The rich also, as a rule, tend to spend more on imports, which does not contribute to GDP. Their consumption pattern is also biased towards luxury goods which typically use capital-intensive methods of production. Employment-generating power of these commodities and services is relatively low.

Most empirical studies conclude that countries with less equal distribution of income, other things equal, tend to grow more slowly. A plausible channel of causation is that increasing returns to scale requires a broad market of middle-class consumers, and a more equal society will have a larger middle class.

Economic growth is generally associated with reduction in poverty. There is evidence that the poverty-reducing power of output growth is lower for more unequal societies where the elite have more power to block redistributive action.

Even Adam Smith, the original proponent of the invisible hand, was in favour of some distribution of wealth from the rich to the poor via progressive taxation. To quote from his *The Wealth of Nations*:

> The necessaries of life occasion the great expense of the poor … The luxuries and vanities of life occasion the principal expense of the rich. It is not very unreasonable that the rich should contribute to the public expense, not only in proportion to their revenue, but something more than in that proportion.

The high saving of the rich and the super-rich is posing a threat from another angle. Return on capital in the real sectors in the developed countries has fallen far behind that in the FIRE (finance, insurance and real estate) sector, where supervision is often weak and non-transparent instruments are continuously being designed (mostly by

American Financial Institutions) to exploit regulatory loopholes. No wonder then that high saving of the rich from all over the world is finding its way to Wall Street in search of higher returns. But financial markets are generally very fragile, driven by bouts of optimism and pessimism unrelated to real causes. Through financial globalisation, this fragility is internationally transmitted at lightning speed. The GFC provides the most glaring example to date. A less skewed distribution of wealth will contribute to stability by lowering the flood of funds into risky financial assets.

The steep rise in inequality in recent decades may be attributed to three major factors.

a Skill-biased technological change
The Third Industrial Revolution (roughly 1970–2000) applied the digital revolution to manufacturing involving the wide use of computers and electronics in home and at work. It ushered in an era where technological change displays a distinctive skill bias. The composition of labour demand, particularly for new products and services, shifted away drastically from semi-skilled labour.

Education has failed to keep pace with this changing demand for skills. Those who already have the high-end skills or manage to acquire them quickly earn much higher returns than those without such skills. Job polarisation has become the dominant feature of labour markets everywhere.

This will become even more prominent with the advent of artificial intelligence (AI) in business operations. Even in the developing countries, the dynamic modern sectors have already adopted the modern skill-intensive technology leading to a scenario of jobless growth. In the near future, AI is most likely to destroy jobs in the middle-skill range like accountancy and other activities where maintaining records, processing information and doing calculations or making forecasts are important. But over longer runs, expanding swathes of services rendered even by expert professionals will begin to disappear. To counter the threat, the demand for elite education focusing on high-level skills may be expected to rise at an accelerated pace. Cost of such education will also rise as a consequence. The poor and the very poor working at the lowest skill rungs might survive the onslaught, but the middle class will be under tremendous pressure. Well-thought-out government action in training and re-training the workforce to cope with the challenge is called for. But financing will remain a serious problem.

India's growth rate in recent years has been quite impressive, significantly above the global average. But the employment scenario in the formal sector continues to be dismal. AI will only make it worse.

b Outsourcing to take advantage of cheap labour. Traditional manufacturing and construction are the only activities that gave employment to semi-skilled or unskilled workers. But the companies of the developed countries have shifted their production or assembling to China, Mexico, the Philippines and other countries where wages and labour standards are much lower than at home. China has emerged as the 'factory of the world'. Its gain has been at the cost of workers at the low end of skills in the developed nations.
c Labour market reforms ruthlessly promoted by the WB and the IMF have weakened the bargaining power of labour considerably. Minimum wages have been abolished or substantially lowered, and pro-labour interventions by national governments in all forms drastically curtailed. As a result, the rate of return on capital has soared with no noticeable improvement in real wages. Median real wage in the private sector in the USA has remained virtually stagnant since the 1980s.

Important work by Thomas Piketty and Joseph Stiglitz, among others, has intensely scrutinised the dynamics of income and wealth inequality in Western capitalist societies over long periods. There is a big literature on the northward movement of inequality in India (Piketty et al., 2024; Ghatak, Raghavan and Xu, 2022).

Apart from income or wealth inequality, there is considerable divergence in regional development, particularly in the developing world. There is also the important issue of gender inequality in all parts of the world. State-level intervention is essential for attacking these problems.

Public policy for inequality reduction should involve progressive taxation of income and wealth and using the funds to carry out necessary action. But in most societies, the political power of the elite and corruption of officials stand in the way of such policy. But it isn't true that nothing can be done. Conditional cash transfer schemes have been effective in putting curb on inequality in Latin America. Such schemes give income support on the condition that some social policy criteria are met, like sending children to school. Fiscal prudence should involve cap on the growth of unproductive spending like frequent salary hikes or huge bonuses for well-paid public sector employees. Subsidies for protecting the standard of living of the poor are 'productive' because they counter the force of rising inequality.

Capital market imperfections of various sorts (calling for high-value collaterals for loans or strict limits on credit or charging higher interest rates, for example) are major hurdles that prevent the poor's access to funds necessary for general education or acquisition of appropriate skills. The state must step in to ease these constraints. Although manufacturing of labour-intensive activities has been outsourced on a big scale to many developing countries, labour market reforms there have ensured that labour's share in the income generated remains low. The 'flexibility' of the labour market must be reversed to some extent. This is not to say that the old days of militant trade unionism should be brought back. That is another extreme to be avoided, because that encourages capital flight and shutting down of business. The tragic industrial decline of the Indian state of West Bengal under communist rule over the period 1979–2013 is a strong reminder of the negative effects of such flight on labour's welfare. There must be a middle ground, which the state should explore and implement in labour market policy.

Insulation against heightened vulnerability

Globalisation has enhanced the level of economic uncertainty due to greater exposure to global shocks over which there is no control at the national level. Needless to say, the poor suffer much more than the richer sections from the increased volatility in their income streams. The government's role is essential in developing coping mechanisms and providing safety nets for the losers in the march of liberalisation and openness. Widespread protests across the globe calling for 'globalisation with a human face' are increasing in frequency and intensity. In his book, *The Crisis of Global Capitalism: Open Society Endangered,* George Soros, who cannot be called a socialist by any stretch of that term, has stated that market fundamentalism is a cruel, predatory system which can be modified and humanised.

Another type of vulnerability is system-wide, not restricted to the poor alone. This has origin in the collapse of asset prices in the financial sector (beginning usually in Wall Street, USA) and the spread of resulting panic across national borders. Entire financial structures (and national economies with them) can be brought to the verge of collapse, as demonstrated by the GFC. Causes of the catastrophe have been examined and re-examined ad infinitum, but there is consensus that sweeping deregulation of finance and unsupervised trade in highly risky assets like securities backed by sub-prime housing mortgages have played a crucial role. The unregulated shadow banking system in the USA was a central player in the tragic drama. Corrupt practices of local commercial banks under weak supervision were among the major factors behind the Asian Crisis of 1997 too.

In response to the GFC, the Dodd–Frank Act was passed in the USA in 2010 in an attempt to curb the power of banks and shadow banks to indulge in socially harmful practices. Fierce lobbying by banks has succeeded in watering down considerably the scope and seriousness of the attempt. Financial Stability Oversight Council, an inter-agency group has also been set up, but so far it has done very little to firewall the US economy against future financial sector risk. Much vaunted macro-prudential policies (caps on loan-to-value ratio, debt-to-income ratio and other prudential measures) to reduce systemic risk have remained mostly on paper. The situation is somewhat better in Europe, but there are clear signs that a handful of big banks in the advanced countries have regained their pre-crisis power to destabilise nations. In search of profit, American banks are once again lending significant amounts to low-quality borrowers saddled with high pre-existing debt. The production of non-transparent instruments cleverly designed to dodge regulation is back on track. Fragility of the FIRE sector remains high and will not come down unless returns increase substantially in the real sector and regulatory oversight becomes stricter. Chances are slim for these two conditions to be met in the near future.

Thanks to RBI's close supervision of domestic banks in transactions involving foreign financial instruments, India was not seriously hurt by the GFC or the earlier Asian crisis. Global financial crises are certain to recur, and despite RBI's insulation, GDP and employment in India will face serious downturns. GoI must stay prepared to meet that contingency.

Taking care of the environment and other components

In spite of its serious shortcomings as a measure of a nation's welfare, GDP and its growth continue to be almost the sole basis for judging a nation's performance and for determining its global ranking. The crucial issue of sustainability of growth over the long run gets scant attention.

Several supplementary measures have been proposed to overcome GDP's limitations as an index of national welfare. In 2010, a committee headed by Amartya Sen, Joseph Stiglitz and Jean Fitoussi suggested a dashboard approach in which several indicators covering financial, natural and human wealth and inequality in distribution are to be carefully monitored. But most economists and environmental experts think that even this attempt is inadequate for assessing growth from the point of view of sustainability, which demands that the interests of future generations be brought more explicitly into the calculations.

Economists have come up with the concept of 'comprehensive wealth' in this context. This encompasses, in addition to physical capital (roads, ports, machinery), human capital (health, education, population size and composition), natural capital (natural resources, ecosystems) and even cultural capital (trust, social norms). There should be balance sheets of national wealth which will show the net change in the stock of this comprehensive wealth over time. GDP growth is sustainable only if it does not make this net change negative.

Constructing comprehensive wealth indicators at national level is statistically not at all easy. But neither was GDP before the government asked for it.

Governments should get rid of, or at least dilute to a significant extent, their current obsession with GDP growth and recognise the need to ensure through checks and balances and regulatory powers that sustainability gets its due share of attention. Carbon taxes and other penalties must be there to cover environmental externalities, as well as curbs on commercial sales promotion that encourage the consumption of status goods that keep people working on hedonic treadmills without doing anything to promote human well-being in the long run.

The Intergovernmental Panel on Climate Change (IPCC), set up in 1988, reports regularly on climate change and the environmental impact of economic activities. Without penalties imposed by governments for harmful actions or rewards for innovations in greener production methods, the private sector cannot be trusted to take environmental concerns seriously.

The vast majority of EU's agricultural subsidies support meat and dairy farming rather than plant alternatives. The supported activities are the main drivers of greenhouse gas emissions, water consumption and air and water pollution. Measures to move towards more environment-friendly provisions face stiff opposition from lobby groups dominated by big farmers. The Green EU policy has actually been watered down in recent years, to the consternation of environmental activists in Europe and elsewhere.

Starting in 2006, the Dutch government substantially reduced the sales tax and road tax on electric and hybrid cars. The result was most encouraging. Over 2006–2012, CO_2 emissions fell substantially. The EU norm of CO_2 emissions was achieved ahead of schedule, and ahead of the rest of Europe, in 2011. But subsequently, due to mounting pressure on revenues, the incentives had to be rolled back substantially, leading to a fall in the sale of green cars. Relaxing the tight caps on permissible budget deficits may partially solve this problem.

A serious coordination problem merits discussion at this point. If a single country goes for punitive measures against industries harming the environment, capitalist owners will not lose much time to move their business elsewhere. This may be costly for the country in terms of lost output, government revenue and employment. Therefore, effective international agreement is critical for effective national policies. But getting political support for an effective international environmental agreement is far from easy, given the political clout of business groups opposed to environmental policies. In 2009, the USA and China joined forces to prevent a meaningful climate agreement to succeed the earlier Kyoto agreement. Developing countries like Brazil, China and India are reluctant to implement anti-pollution rules and regulations. After all, why should they listen to the rich countries who freely exploited nature in the past and continue to do so in the present?

Fostering innovation

Another area where governments have played a significant role in fostering long-term growth is research and development (R&D). The image of very agile private enterprise doing research independent of the clumsy, at best non-interfering, state leviathan is simply wrong. Historically, the state has been and still is important for innovations in the USA. Much of Apple's success depends on state grants for R&D

in the information, communication and technology (ICT) sector. The state provides public capital in areas considered too risky by private venture capital. There are major instances in US history where private capital followed public venture capital fifteen or twenty years later.

The Internet did not fall out of the sky of summertime California. It was built by the government. The US government spent about $125 million building its predecessors. In the 1960s and 1970s, the US Army sponsored research on how to link computers to enable sharing of data. This made possible a network of university computers. The Silicon Valley continues to prosper through private–public synergy. Crucial breakthroughs were also made at the European Laboratory for Particle Physics (CERN in French acronym), a cooperative effort of European governments. (In the USA, direct government control of the Internet ended only in 1995.)

India's success story in ICT and service exports (based chiefly in Bengaluru, Hyderabad and Tamil Nadu) is also the product of government–business collaboration.

Global pharmaceutical companies are heavily dependent on government support. Research for the COVID-19 vaccine couldn't have happened in competitive markets ruled by the invisible hand. Enabling policies of GoI during the pre-reform decades have been crucial for the success of Indian pharmaceutical companies, such as Lupin, Ranbaxy and Dr Reddy's Laboratories.

This type of fruitful private–public partnership in the field of technological research must continue. Dogmatic insistence on fiscal prudence must not stand in the way.

Emerging patterns of fiscal plans across countries show that these issues are getting much more attention than they used to get in the past. The one-size-fits-all approach is giving way to more attention to each country's specific context. While retaining the stress on debt reduction and deficit management, new rules approved by the European Parliament are designed to make fiscal operations clearer, more flexible and better tailored to the situations of the member countries. New benchmark ratios have been introduced to monitor the debt situation more closely. Social concerns have received wider coverage. These changes in content and orientation are not confined to the EU alone.

Switzerland has adopted an expenditure rule under which planned federal government spending cannot exceed projected receipts multiplied by a business cycle adjustment factor. The adjustment factor is set above unity in bad times (relaxing the constraint on spending) and below unity (tightening the constraint) if inflation and other symptoms of overheating appear as a threat. This Swiss innovation deserves to be adopted more widely.

The commendable success in fighting the GFC and the pandemic, the two terrible catastrophes of recent history, was due in no small measure to successful global coordination of tax-spending (and monetary) policies. Important lessons have been learnt, which should be handy if and when similar disasters threaten to materialise once more.

Global coordination is also needed to address the issue of tax havens. Rich people have the option of taking their money out of the country and into tax havens if they face higher income or wealth tax. Given the clout of wealth in politics everywhere, it is very unlikely that the need will get adequate attention in global forums in the near future.

A very important issue confronting fiscal policy in today's world concerns the impact of demographic change on the resources of governments.

Fiscal policy in an ageing society

Dependency ratio (excluding children) in a society is defined as follows:

α = number of people receiving income transfers/number of people financing that transfer

Among all possible types of transfer, we shall focus on the intergenerational transfer from the young (workers) to the old (retired persons). Apart from purely private arrangements, governments play an important role here by taxing the young and transferring the funds to retired persons.

Under a pay-as-you-go scheme, taxes collected from the working generation are used to support the consumption needs of the older generation. There is no private wealth accumulation for this purpose. The sustainability of the scheme depends critically on movements in the dependency ratio α.

The ratio α increases if (i) people take earlier retirement, (ii) longevity rises due to improvements in health standards and (iii) birth rate declines, reducing the size of the working-age population. It is easy to see that with unchanged tax rates and income of the productive generation, each retired person will receive less income transfer as α increases. And in most of the developed countries, where social security and healthcare provision constitute the two major government programmes to support the elderly, α is indeed rising steadily over time. This is putting government finances under severe pressure in those countries.

In the face of rising α, the following measures are usually adopted: (a) raising the tax revenue by raising the tax rate or the tax base, (b) pushing back the age of retirement and (c) cutting down the retirement benefits (in systems where designated retirement benefits prevail). Items (b) and (c) fall under the broad head of pension reforms, which are being very vigorously researched by public finance experts of the world.

Higher taxation will have disincentive effect on labour supply. Lower retirement benefits, on the other hand, may induce young people to work harder and earn more in order to offset the expected decline in future income flows. The net effect on current labour force participation is ambiguous. Precautionary saving may rise, dampening the growth of current spending. Higher saving, however, may not be an option for the poorer sections whose employment status is precarious and who suffer disproportionately from serious capital market imperfections. If application of AI in production adds to the society's pool of unemployment, cost of social safety nets will go up. At the same time, it may boost tax revenue by raising output per worker in the current period.

Since raising taxation is always politically unpopular, governments may be tempted to finance rising social security costs by printing money (borrowed from central banks). The possible inflationary impact will be muted or absent if simultaneously there is growth in the productivity of young workers to counteract the relative fall in their numbers. AI may be of help here.

Fiscal authorities must find a viable solution to the serious challenge posed by demographic and technological changes.

9 Conclusion

In the course of this short book, we have taken a tour of the major issues surrounding the appropriate role of the government (a non-private agent with power to formulate and enforce rules) in the economy keeping the main focus on budgetary or fiscal action. The major arguments advanced over centuries for and against the pro-active role of the state in the spheres of allocation, stabilisation and distribution have been laid out and assessed. The uses and abuses of fiscal power have received due attention.

The evolution of fiscal policy in India since independence has been briefly sketched, and the major drawbacks (such as the acute regressiveness of tax instruments and socially wasteful subsidies) are pointed out.

It has been demonstrated repeatedly over the past half-century that a free market economy (where the state plays only an enabling role through supply-side policies that stop at enhancing the profitability of business operations) advocated by the conservative school cannot solve the very serious problems of large-scale unemployment of labour, persistent poverty, widening inequality in distribution of income and wealth and unsustainable growth of GDP that gives scant attention to the health of the natural environment. Regulation is absolutely essential to alleviate these ills, but not in the crude, heavy-handed way of the past. Government failure is an undeniable reality, the government being a man-made institution after all. But the solution lies in reforming the institution to improve its performance, not in tying it up hand and foot. Fiscal (or monetary) discipline is certainly desirable, but not at the cost of socially useful public expenditure that

DOI: 10.4324/9781003585404-10

pays due attention to the welfare of the less privileged sections and of unborn future generations.

'Laissez-faire' is a French phrase that means 'allow to do' or, in more expanded form, 'let the people do what they choose to do'. A laissez-faire economy is an alternative name for the type of purely self-interest-driven economy that the conservatives insistently praise and demand. We end with the wise words of Keynes expressed in his book, *The End of Laissez-Faire*, published in 1926:

> I think that capitalism, wisely managed, can probably be made more efficient for attaining economic ends than any alternative system yet in sight, but that in itself it is in many ways extremely objectionable.

Through our discussion, we hope to have persuaded the reader of the essential truth of this assertion. 'Market versus the state' is a false way of approaching the problem of managing an economy. The market, which is an immensely intricate and useful institution built up by human beings over centuries, must be judiciously governed to promote the welfare of citizens. Governments should be good enough to deliver good governance using all the policy tools at their command.

Bibliography

Ahluwalia, MS, Economic reforms in India since 1991: has gradualism worked? *Journal of Economic Perspectives*, 16, 3, 2002.

Atkinson, AB and Stiglitz, J, The design of tax structure: direct versus indirect taxation, *Journal of Public Economics*, 6, 1976.

Bagchi, A, Fiscal policy for financing development: the Indian experience, in Kapila, U (ed) *Indian Economy Since Independence*, 1999, Academic Foundation.

Barro, R, Are government bonds net wealth? *Journal of Political Economy*, 82, 1095–1117, December 1974.

Barro, R and Sala-I-Martin, X, Public finance in models of economic growth, *Review of Economic Studies*, 59, 1992.

Barwell, R, *Macroeconomic Policy after the Crash: Issues in Monetary and Fiscal Policy*, Palgrave McMillan, 2016.

Bhattacharyya, R, Ghosh Dastidar, A and Sikdar, S, *The Covid-19 Pandemic, India and the World*, Routledge, 2022.

Buchanan, JM, Tollison, RD and Tullock, G, (ed) *Toward a Theory of the Rent-Seeking Society*, Texas A&M University Press, 1980.

Chakrabarti, P and Gupta, S, Changing dynamics of intergovernmental fiscal relations in India, in Sikdar, S (ed) *The Post-Reform Indian Economy: An Unfolding Story*, Orient Black Swan, 2023.

Chattopadhyay, S, *Macroeconomics of the Black Economy*, Orient Black Swan, 2018.

Coase, R, The problem of social cost, *The Journal of Law and Economics*, 3, 1960.

Dales, JH, *Pollution, Property and Prices*, University of Toronto Press, 1968.

Dasgupta, A, Ghosh, S, Mookherjee, D, Tax administration reform and tax-payer compliance in India, *International Tax and Public Finance*, 11, 2004.

Economic Surveys, GoI, RBI reports, various issues, GoI.

Evensky, J, *Adam Smith's Moral Philosophy: A Historical and Contemporary Perspective on Markets, Law, Ethics and Culture*, Cambridge University Press, 2005.

Ferhr, H, Jokisch, S and Kotlikoff, LJ, The world's interconnected demographic/fiscal transition, *Journal of the Economics of Ageing*, 1–2, 2013.

Fisher, D. *Monetary and Fiscal Policy*, MacMillan, 1988.

Galbraith, JK, *The Affluent Society*, 4th edition, Houghton Miff, 1984.

Ghatak, M, Raghavan, R and Xu, L, *Trends in Economic Inequality in India*, The India Forum, 2022.

Grampp, WD, What did Smith mean by the invisible hand? *Journal of Political Economy*, 108, 2000.

Gupta, R, Khere, R and Narayanan, S, Minimum support price in India: distilling the facts, *Review of Agrarian Studies*, 2, 2021.

Hayek, F, *The Road to Serfdom*, Routledge, 1944.

Hayek, F, *The Fatal Conceit: The Errors of Socialism*, new edition, University of Chicago Press, 1988.

Heer, B, Polito, V and Wickens, MR, Population ageing, social security and fiscal limits, *Journal of Economic Dynamics and Control*, 116, 1–27, July 2020.

Jawed Akhtar, SM and Naseem, S, *Fiscal Reforms in India since 1991*, New Century Publications, 2013.

Keynes, JM, *The End of Laissez Faire, 1926, The General Theory of Employment, Interest and Money*, MacMillan, 1936.

Khan, NA, *Challenges and Issues in Fiscal Federalism*, Springer, 2018.

Kitao, S, Policy uncertainty and cost of delayed reform: the case of ageing Japan, *Review of Economic Dynamics*, 27, 2018.

Kumar, A, *Understanding the Black Economy and Black Money in India: An Enquiry into the Causes, Consequences and Remedies*, Aleph Spotlight, 2017.

Larch, M and Martins, JN, *Fiscal Policy in the European Union: An Assessment of Current Practice and Challenges*, Routledge, 2009.

Marsiliani, L, Rauscher, M and Withagen, C, *Environmental Policy and the International Economy*, Kluwer Academic Publishers, 2002.

McCaffery, EJ and Slemrod, J (ed), *Behavioral Public Finance*, Russell Sage Foundation, 2006.

McMillan, J, *Reinventing the Bazaar: A Natural History of Markets*, W.W. Norton and Company, 2002.

Mundle, S (ed), *Public Finance in India*, Oxford University Press, New Delhi, 1997.

Pigou, AC, *The Economics of Welfare*, McMillan, 1920.

Piketty, T, *Capital in the Twenty-First Century*, Harvard University Press, 2014.

Piketty, T, Bharti, NK, Chancel, L and Somanchi, A, *Income and Wealth Inequality in India 1922–2023, The Rise of the Billionaire Raj*, World Inequality Lab, 2024.

Piketty, T and Saez, E, Income inequality in the United States, 1913–1998, *Quarterly Journal of Economics*, 115, 1, 2003.

Rakshit, M, *Macroeconomics of Post-Reform India*, Oxford University Press, 2009.

Ramaswami, B, *Agricultural Subsidies: Study Prepared for XV Finance Commission*, Indian Statistical Institute, 2019.

Reddy, YV, Ray, P and Valluri, N, *Financial and Fiscal Policies: Crises and New Realities*, Oxford University Press, 2014.

Reinhart, C and Rogoff, K, *This Time Is Different: Eight Centuries of Financial Folly*, Harvard University Press, 2008.

Sen, A, *Development as Freedom*, Alfred A Knopf, 1999.

Serra, N and Stiglitz, J (ed) *The Washington Consensus Reconsidered; Towards a New Global Governance*, Oxford University Press, 2008.

Shome, P, *India's Fiscal Matters*, Oxford University Press, 2002.

Sikdar, S and Chakrabarti, D, Fiscal policy in India: overview of some major issues, in Chatterjee, B and Sasmal, J (ed) *The Indian Economy @75: Successes and Challenges*, Routledge, 2024.

Singh, AK, Fiscal reforms in India since 1991: a critical assessment, *Indian Journal of Public Administration*, 50, 2004.

Skidelsky, R, *The Road from Serfdom: The Economic and Political Consequences of the End of Communism*, Penguin, 1996.

Slemrod, J (ed), *Does Atlas Shrug? The Economic Consequences of Taxing the Rich*, Harvard University Press, 2000.

Smith, A, *An Inquiry into the Nature and Causes of The Wealth of Nations*, University of Chicago Press, 1976, originally published in 1776.

Soros, G, *The Crisis of Global Capitalism*, Hachette Book Group, 1998.

Stern, N, *The Economics of Climate Change: The Stern Review*, Cambridge University Press, 2007.

Stiglitz, J, *The Price of Inequality: How Today's Divided Society Endangers Our Future*, W.W. Norton, 2012.

Stiglitz, J, *The Road to Freedom: Economics and the Good Society*, Penguin, Random House, 2024.

Tullock, G, The welfare costs of monopoly, tariffs and theft, *Western Economic Journal*, 5, 1967.

Tullock, G, *The Economics of Special Privilege and Rent Seeking*, Kluwer Academic Publishers, 1988.

Winer, SL and Shibata, H (ed), *Political Economy and Public Finance*, Edward Elgar, 2003.

World Inequality Database, *World Development Reports*, World Bank.

Index

FSC
www.fsc.org
MIX
Papier | Fördert gute Waldnutzung
FSC® C083411

Kolibri 360 GmbH
Ferdinand-Jühlke-Straße 7
99095 Erfurt, Deutschland
produktsicherheit@kolibri360.de